Painting Floral Botanicals

Wild Lupine

Sage

Nasturtium

MICHELLE TEMARES

NORTH LIGHT BOOKS
Cincinnati, Ohio
www.artistsnetwork.com

D1275287

About the Author

Michelle Temares is a noted designer, writer, speaker and teacher, as well as the principal of Design Innovations Inc., a product development and design firm serving the home furnishings, giftware and hobby industries. Products Michelle has designed are offered at major department and specialty stores throughout the United States and Europe.

Although Michelle's design activities span a wide range, her first love remains decorative painting. She teaches and lectures at national decorative painting conventions, at chapter meetings of the Society of Decorative Painters and at her own Bella Michelle Studios in Garden City, New York.

This is Michelle's first book for North Light Books. She is delighted to be able to bring some of the joy of painting floral botanicals to people she hasn't had the opportunity to teach in person.

Other fine North Light Books are available from your local bookstore or art supply store or direct from the publisher.

05 04 03 02 01   5 4 3 2 1
Library of Congress Cataloging-in-Publication Data
Temares, Michelle.
    Painting floral botanicals / Michelle Temares.
        p. cm.
    Includes bibliographical references (p.).
    ISBN 1-58180-072-X (pbk. : alk. paper)
      1. Botanical illustration--Technique. 2. Acrylic painting--Technique. I. Title.

    QK98.24 .T46 2001
    758'.42--dc21   00-065363

Edited by Jennifer Long and Maureen Mahany Berger
Production coordinated by Emily Gross
Cover design by Stephanie Strang
Interior design by Lisa Buchanan
Page layout by Kathy Bergstrom
Materials photographed by Christine Polomsky
Finished artwork photographed by Al Parrish

Dedication

To my mother,
Phyllis Dolin Falk,
who also never gave up.

Acknowledgments

First and foremost, my endless and eternal thanks to Mark Evan Temares. Without his support and encouragement this book, and in fact my entire design career, would not have been possible.

Special thanks also to the following:
- Kathy Kipp, who gave me a chance and provided invaluable guidance.
- Jennifer Long, whose insight has been critical to my success.
- Susan Monahan, who took a risk on me early in my career when no one else was willing to.
- Shirley Miller, who has led me down the right path on many occasions.
- Neal and Bobbie Pearcy, for their ongoing support.
- Faith Wismer, for her ongoing support.
- Chris Wallace, for her professionalism and support.
- Paul Baumgarten, for his expert legal counsel.
- Mike Hartnett, for his support and friendship.
- Susan Reitman, Eileen Mislove and Ed Seltzer for giving me the tools to do the job.
- Caren Falk Lucas, for her encouragement and belief in me.
- Veta Sheppard-Hayes and Mary Gundolfi Ratzel for loving me anyway.

Thank you also to the following companies whose quality products have been used in this book:

Alto's EZ Mat, Inc.

Barb Watson's Brushworks

Crescent Cardboard Co., L.L.C.

Hy-Jo Picture Frames

Krylon

Loew-Cornell

Masterson Art Products, Inc.

Plaid Enterprises, Inc.

Therm O Web, Inc.

Viking Woodcrafts

Walnut Hollow Farm, Inc.

Winsor & Newton

Table of Contents

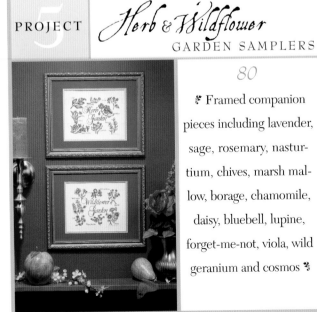
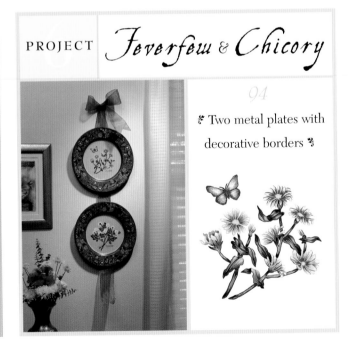

PROJECT 3 | *Spring Bulbs*

54

❦ A metal bowl with daffodils, tulips and hyacinths ❦

PROJECT 4 | *Morning Glory & Sweet Pea*

66

❦ Framed companion pieces with decorative borders ❦

PROJECT 7 | *Peony*

106

❦ A painted wooden tray ❦

PROJECT 8 | *Iris & Columbine*

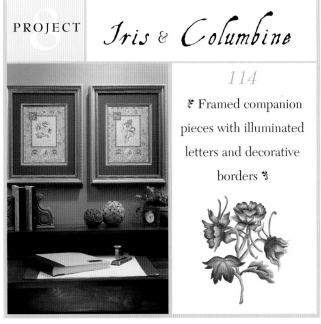

114

❦ Framed companion pieces with illuminated letters and decorative borders ❦

Introduction

THE ORIGINS OF BOTANICAL ILLUSTRATION

Long before photography, television and the Internet provided instant pictures, there was a desperate need for realistic renderings of all natural subjects, including herbs and flowers. The need was particularly great in the scientific and medical communities, where herbs and flowers were of potential value for food and medicine. Knowledge that could not be passed along in person could best be passed along with an accurate illustration.

Botanical illustrations have been used throughout history, with the illustrative style reflecting their historical and geographical origin. Early depictions were simple woodcuts without much detail. More elaborate illustrations became available in the fifteenth and sixteenth centuries with the advent of improved printing techniques and movable type.

Until the age of the explorers, botanical illustrations traveled relatively short distances. The illustrations were only useful if the herb or flower was available in the local area. Once trading routes became active, botanical art began to travel the world as it documented species never before seen outside of native climates. As leisure travel became easier in the eighteenth and nineteenth centuries, artists had new opportunities to explore and document species from all over the world.

The increased availability of plants from near and far led to an explosion in the popularity of botanical art across all levels of society. Marie Antoinette, Queen of France, employed a botanical illustrator, Pierre-Joseph Redoute, just to document her gardens. Hundreds of years later, his beautiful and graceful illustrations remain among the most loved botanical prints.

Botanical illustration also became a wildly popular hobby among middle-class women; this interest continued until the end of the Victorian era.

FLOWER PAINTINGS VERSUS BOTANICAL ILLUSTRATIONS

Are all flower paintings also botanical illustrations? The answer is no. While many paintings of flowers may be extremely beautiful, they do not qualify as floral botanicals unless certain criteria are met. The hallmark of any botanical painting is its realism and accurate depiction of the subject's growth habit, flower, leaf, stem and sometimes roots. The true botanical artist is so committed to accuracy that he or she will even study the floral sample under a magnifying glass, sometimes dissecting parts with tweezers for further analytical study. In botanical illustration, the correct leaf must appear on the depicted flower, relative size between elements must be accurate, the number and structure of petals must be correct and the color must match the sample as closely as possible. The final illustration must also be aesthetically pleasing in composition, technique and color.

THE REVIVAL OF BOTANICAL ILLUSTRATION

While botanical illustration never fully died, photography did substantially dampen demand for it. However, in the past few years botanical illustrations, and particularly floral botanicals, have undergone a tremendous revival. Prices for antique prints have skyrocketed, and work by contemporary artists is also experiencing steady price increases.

The revival of botanical art has been heavily fueled by our increasing need to make our homes beautiful refuges from the outside world. No longer do these captivating masterpieces stay buried in reference books for scholars. Now they find their equally rightful place on the walls of our homes. In the past, the accuracy of botanical art was its most important element. Today accuracy is a close second only to decorative value. The classic, natural subject matter works beautifully in traditional and country decorating schemes, as well as in contemporary decor. A botanical's versatility within the home is also quite remarkable. Living rooms, family rooms, dining rooms, bedrooms and garden rooms can all be enhanced with the addition of botanical paintings.

PAINTING FLORAL BOTANICALS

This book gives you the opportunity to create and enjoy your own floral botanicals. The step-by-step instructions and photographs, along with the patterns and color charts, will allow you to create paintings for your use in your own home.

I encourage you also to spend some time with the chapter on drawing flowers and begin to try your hand at creating your own original floral botanicals. With time and patience, you will be amazed at your success and you will feel richly rewarded by your accomplishments.

To appeal to your different painting moods and needs, the projects in this book cover a wide range of approaches. Some are traditional botanicals painted on a white background, such as the Bleeding Heart and Wild Roses projects. Other projects capture the spirit of the art, yet incorporate a more decorative approach, using less traditional botanical composition and colorings. All projects, however, share one common trait: The core characteristics of botanical art are always retained. The complete and accurate depiction of flower, leaf and stem is a part of every project.

CONTACT ME

A book like this is primarily a labor of love. My hope is that it adds relaxation and enjoyment to your life. Please feel free to write to me with comments or suggestions, or to request information about travel teaching:

Michelle Temares
472 Old Country Rd.
Garden City, NY 11530
USA
E-mail: mft@iname.com

Paint with love and peace and it will extend into your life.

Most sincerely,

Supplies

CORE SUPPLIES

The joys of an art supply store! Nothing gets my heart and creativity racing like a visit to my neighborhood art store. Suddenly, a five-minute stop for a paint refill turns into an hour-long, art-induced high. Yes, I am an art supply junkie.

Throughout my career I have experimented with countless supplies, and I continue to try new products as they are introduced. Over the years I have found several products that I just can't do without. These are the products I used in this book. They are readily available and continually produce excellent results. However, many other brands are available at your local supply stores. So, please use whatever you're comfortable with.

WATERCOLOR PAPER

I painted several of the projects in this book on watercolor paper. My students are often surprised that they can use acrylic paint successfully on watercolor paper. One of the many benefits of experimenting with your materials is that you may find uses and results that you never thought possible.

The watercolor paper I used in this book is Winsor & Newton 140-lb. (300gsm) cold-press. The 140-lb. refers to the weight of a ream (500 sheets) of the paper. The 140-lb. paper is a good midrange, versatile weight. It is heavy enough to withstand several layers of paint but light enough to be translucent when placed over a lightbox to transfer a drawing.

Cold-press refers to the texture. Watercolor paper is made in three textures: hot-press, cold-press and rough. Hot-press paper has a smooth finish, rough has a bumpy finish and cold-press is right in the middle with a slightly textured surface.

The paper is available in both block and loose sheet form. Blocks of paper are glued together at the sides, and loose sheets come in 22" × 30" (55.9cm × 76.2cm) sheets. Either is fine.

Most watercolor papers need to be soaked and stretched before they can be used for painting, or the moisture will cause them to buckle. Winsor & Newton paper is unique because it is both internally and externally sized. This results in a paper that does not have to be soaked or stretched. It's ready to use as soon as you bring it home. It will remain flat regardless of the number of layers of paint you apply.

Removing Mistakes

I discovered another advantage of Winsor & Newton's watercolor paper completely by accident. I was under a tight deadline and realized that the artwork was not progressing well. There was no time for a redo and corrections on watercolor paper are rarely successful. Attempts to scrub out a mistake usually result in an obvious uneven texture, or worse, holes in the artwork. Feeling I had nothing to lose, I began to attempt to slowly lift color with a damp cotton swab. The paint slowly began to lift without damaging the paper. After allowing the area to dry, I repainted it. No corrections were noticeable. I know of no other watercolor paper that will allow this type of correction. Paint with confidence.

BOTTLED ACRYLIC PAINT

I painted all of the projects in this book with Plaid FolkArt acrylic paints. FolkArt paint has several qualities that make it my preferred brand of bottled acrylic paint.

- It has excellent coverage. Therefore, only one basecoat is usually necessary when using the techniques in this book. Highlights and shades build faster as well.
- It has a creamy consistency, which allows for smooth layering.
- The colors intermix beautifully, which means fewer colors need to be purchased.

BLENDING GEL

Plaid makes several mediums for use with FolkArt paint. Blending Gel, which I used extensively throughout the book, allows the acrylics to blend easily without diluting the pigment or changing the color.

BRUSHES

While almost any brush will perform well the first few times you use it, the real test of a quality brush is how it performs over time. A quality brush will maintain a sharp point, retain its spring and continue to hold a good volume of paint, allowing for less frequent reloading.

I painted all of the projects in this book with Loew-Cornell brushes. I have had some of my Loew-Cornell brushes in constant use for almost ten years, yet they still paint as well now as they did when they were brand new. With proper care your brushes can last just as long.

Brushes are primarily divided into two categories: natural hair and synthetic. The preferred natural hair is sable. The sable brushes I used in this book are from Loew-Cornell's Art Tec line. These brushes maintain a sharp point while holding a good quantity of paint. A sharp point is especially important when doing the lettering that accompanies many of the projects.

Save these more expensive sable brushes for the projects painted on watercolor paper. The other surfaces have rougher finishes and can wear out the sable brushes rather quickly. For the non-paper projects use the La Corneille brushes from Loew-Cornell. These synthetic hair brushes perform similarly to the sable brushes and will hold up well over time when used on rougher surfaces, such as wood.

Brush Care

Following are a few tips that will help your brushes last for many years:

- ❦ Never allow paint to dry in the brush.
- ❦ Wash the hairs completely when you are finished painting for the day. Use a mild soap or a cleaner made specifically for artists' brushes, rinse several times with clean water and then reshape the hair.
- ❦ Dry the brushes suspended with their bristles pointed down, or hang the brushes over the edge of a counter. This will prevent water from seeping into the handle and causing swelling or splitting.
- ❦ When loading the brush with paint, never load more than three-fourths of the way up the hairs. Any farther and paint may seep into the metal section (called the ferrule). When paint seeps into the ferrule it is almost impossible to remove. As it dries, the bristles will permanently spread and the brush will lose the ability to hold a sharp point or crisp chisel edge.

PALETTE

A Masterson Sta-Wet Palette is very helpful when painting with acrylic paint. Acrylics dry very rapidly; if the paint begins to dry while you are painting, it will be difficult to load the brush and blending will be choppy and unattractive. The Masterson Sta-Wet Palette will keep acrylic paints moist for a minimum of a month. This not only makes painting easier but it is also a money saver because paint is never wasted or thrown out at the end of a session.

The palette consists of a bottom tray, sponge, specially treated palette paper and a lid.

Prepare the palette by immersing the sponge in water. Place the sopping wet sponge in the bottom of the palette. Run the palette paper under very hot water until it is thoroughly wet, then place the paper on top of the sponge. Wipe any puddles off of the top of the palette paper with a paper towel. Now place your paints directly on top of the palette paper.

Every few hours, check that the sponge is still damp. When it begins to dry, pour a small amount of water into the bottom of the palette under the sponge. If you step away from your painting for more than a few minutes, cover the palette with its tight-fitting lid and the paints will remain moist and workable.

CHINA PLATE

I pour my varnish onto a china plate and load my brush from this puddle. The smooth surface of the plate results in fewer air bubbles and a smoother finish. It's best to set aside a plate to use only for painting; a flea market or garage sale find will work just fine.

PALETTE KNIFE

I use the Loew-Cornell no. 609 palette knife for mixing paints on my palette. The compact size of this palette knife makes it easy to handle. It's sharp enough to cut through paint quickly but not so sharp that it will tear through the palette paper.

Fixing Mistakes

If you are a beginning painter, or would like extra security against painting mistakes, keep a damp paper towel on your lap. Mistakes can be quickly wiped away before they dry and become permanent.

Additional Supplies

SUPPLIES FOR PAINTING ON WOOD

❦ Wood sealer.

❦ Foam brushes to apply the sealer.

❦ Wood filler, if needed.

❦ 400-grit sandpaper.

❦ Tack cloth.

❦ Paper towels to blot excess water from brushes. Buy the heaviest paper towels you can find, or try shop towels, available from hardware stores. These towels are even heavier and more absorbent than supermarket paper towels. They cost more, but you will use fewer.

❦ Two water basins. These can be simple glass jars, plastic food containers or the water basins made especially for decorative painting with brush-cleaning ridges on the bottom. Use one basin for cleaning brushes and one for clean water for wet-on-wet techniques. Change the water as soon as it becomes visibly dirty. Dirty water does affect the beauty of the paint.

SUPPLIES FOR TRANSFERRING PATTERNS

❦ Hard pencil (4H or higher) or stylus.

❦ Vinyl eraser.

❦ Tracing paper.

❦ Ruler.

❦ Wax-free transfer paper.

❦ Quality transparent tape.

❦ A lightbox may also be used for transferring to watercolor paper.

FINISHING SUPPLIES

❦ Krylon Workable Fixative, no. 1306. Projects painted on watercolor paper are more damage prone than those painted on hardier surfaces, such as wood or metal. For protection, lightly spray thoroughly dry paintings with Krylon Workable Fixative. This will protect the painting from airborne dust and grime and will also provide protection against runs should the painting accidentally come in contact with water.

❦ Varnish for wood and metal pieces, if desired.

❦ An old toothbrush for spattering.

❦ Cheesecloth and plastic wrap for the background finish on several projects.

DRAWING SUPPLIES

Here are the supplies you will need to get started making your own botanical sketches.

❦ Tracing paper.

❦ 4H pencil or a lead holder with a 4H lead. I prefer the lead holder because the lead stays sharp longer than a regular pencil. This means fewer interruptions to sharpen the pencil, and less sharpening makes it more economical. It also has a more consistent point, resulting in a more consistent drawing.

❦ Rotary sharpener (if using lead holder).

❦ Cork-backed metal ruler.

❦ Vellum graph paper.

❦ T-square.

❦ Vinyl eraser.

Preparing the *Surface* & Transferring the *Pattern*

PREPARING THE SURFACE

This book includes projects painted on paper, metal and wood. The paper and metal need very little preparation, so we'll spend less time on tedious prep work and more time painting.

WATERCOLOR PAPER

Since Winsor & Newton watercolor paper is sized both internally and externally, no preparation is needed. Cut the piece of paper to the dimensions given in the project, which are slightly larger than the pattern. This will provide a margin of error in the event that the edges of the paper become soiled or bent. It will also be more stable and easier to frame because the edges can be affixed directly to the mat.

METALWARE

All of the metal surfaces I used in this book came from Barb Watson's Brushworks. The pieces come preprimed—no cleaning, sealing or sanding is necessary. They are ready to basecoat and paint as soon as they arrive at your door.

WOOD

The secret to the success of a beautifully painted wood piece lies in the preparation. Nothing is more frustrating than investing hours in a project, not to mention the financial investment, only to be disappointed in the final piece because it was not prepped properly. A well-prepared surface will result in a smooth and even finish. Preparation of the wood pieces in this book should take no more than an hour, and it is time well spent.

The wood companies who produce surfaces for the decorative painting industry know the importance of a well-prepped piece. The suppliers included in this book thoroughly sand their pieces before shipping. This dramatically cuts down the sanding that you will need to do once your piece is sealed.

If you are working with rougher wood, follow the same prep instructions but start with a rougher sandpaper, working down to a finer grade for a smooth finish. It will just take a little more elbow grease.

PREPARING WOOD

1 | Use the water-based wood sealer of your choice. Your local craft or art supply retailer should stock several. In a small painting dish or palette, mix the sealer with water in a 1:1 ratio. Stroke the sealer on the wood in the direction of the grain. I prefer to use an inexpensive foam brush to apply the sealer. This saves wear and tear on good painting brushes. Make sure to spread the sealer evenly in corners and over the edges as it has a tendency to well up, leaving unattractive bumps. Smooth out any bumps before the sealer dries. Only one coat is needed.

2 | If the wood has any holes or indentations, fill these with wood filler. Several applications may be needed as the filler sometimes shrinks as it dries. Once the sealer and wood filler are dry, lightly sand the wood until smooth. I prefer a 400-grit sandpaper. Do not oversand. The goal is a smooth but not glass-like finish. If the piece is sanded to a glass-like finish it will have no tooth and the paint will bead up and not adhere to the wood.

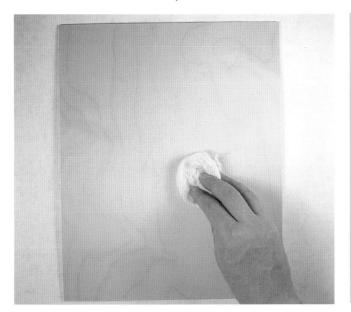

The Benefits of Sealing Wood

Sealing the wood accomplishes several goals. First, any sap still present in the wood will be locked underneath the sealer and will be less likely to bleed through to the finished painting. Second, basecoats will be smoother as the surface is now evenly absorbent. Third, sealed wood is less absorbent and therefore less paint is needed. Finally, the sealer will slightly raise the grain of the wood so it can be sanded smooth. Without the sealer, the painted basecoat would raise the grain, resulting in a bumpy and uneven finish.

3 | Lightly rub a tack cloth (a piece of cheesecloth treated with a sticky resin) over the surface of the wood to remove any grit left from the sandpaper. Look for tack cloths at art supply, craft supply and hardware stores. Remove the cloth carefully from its original wrapper; if placed back into the wrapper and tightly sealed, it will stay usable for at least a year. You are now ready for paint.

Transferring the Pattern

Due to the intricacy of botanical paintings and lettering, an accurate transfer is very important. Please take the time to do the pattern transfer accurately and methodically. You will be much more pleased with your results. It's tedious, but necessary.

The two most accurate methods to transfer patterns to watercolor paper are the lightbox method and the transfer paper method. My personal preference is the lightbox method because it provides the crispest, most accurate and cleanest transfer. The transfer paper method is popular with decorative painters and works on almost any surface, including wood, metal, porcelain and stoneware.

When tracing straight lines such as borders, use a ruler as a guide instead of tracing freehand. The results will be more professional.

1 Make a photocopy of the desired pattern directly from this book. Set the copier on a darker-than-average setting. This will help you to see the pattern through the watercolor paper. Tape the photocopied pattern securely to the lightbox so that it will not shift.

2 Position the watercolor paper over the pattern and tape these edges securely as well.

Lightbox Substitutes

If you do not have a lightbox and would like to try this method, a window on a sunny day can be used as a substitute. If your computer screen is large enough, it will work in a pinch as well. Lay your pattern directly on the window or computer screen and follow the directions below. If you plan to continue to draw or paint on watercolor paper, treat yourself to a lightbox. You will be pleased with the ease of the transfer and the results.

3 Turn on the lightbox. Using a 4H pencil, lightly trace the pattern onto the watercolor paper. Pressing too hard will create a permanent indentation in the paper. Keep the pencil well sharpened, especially when transferring the lettering. It will be much easier to paint from a clean and precise transfer. Shut the lightbox off and make sure you've transferred the entire pattern before removing it from the lightbox. It can be difficult to realign the pattern once it is removed. Carefully remove the tape and the transferred pattern from the lightbox. The transfer should be as light as possible so that pencil lines don't appear in the final painting. If the transfer could be lighter, softly rub a vinyl eraser over it. This will pick up the excess lead without smearing.

THE TRANSFER PAPER METHOD

1 | Trace the pattern from the book directly onto tracing paper. Trace as accurately as possible. Use a ruler for any straight lines, including borders.

2 | Place the painting surface on a clean and flat tabletop. Place the transfer paper, darker side down, onto the surface. Secure with tape. Purchase wax-free transfer paper specifically for art use. Cheaper waxed versions will leave a residue on your surface that is extremely difficult to cover with paint. Place the pattern on top of the transfer paper. Secure this with tape as well.

3 | Using a stylus or 4H pencil, trace the pattern lines onto the surface. Some artists prefer to use a colored pencil or fine pen so that it is easy to see which lines were already transferred. Remember to use a ruler for straight edges. For large or complex pieces, it can be easier and more accurate to transfer the pattern if it is cut into sections. For example, drawer patterns can be transferred separately from cabinet doors, the lip of a bowl or plate can be transferred separately from the center portion.

 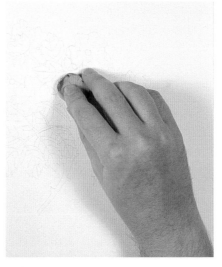

4 | Lift a corner and peek to ensure that the pattern is transferring to the surface. Adjust your pressure accordingly. A light transfer is best. If no transfer lines are visible, be sure you haven't placed the transfer paper upside down. Before completely disassembling the setup, lift small portions and check that all lines were transferred.

5 | The transfer lines should be as light as possible. Lighten the transfer as necessary by softly moving a vinyl eraser over the surface.

Drawing Flowers, Stems & Leaves

6 Steps to Drawing Beautiful and Realistic Flowers

Drawing flowers is relaxing and enjoyable because flowers are so forgiving. Other subjects—portraits for example—require exact precision. If a feature is drawn inaccurately or set into the face incorrectly, the person may look rather odd. Flowers, however, allow more room for error. If the drawn leaf leans slightly more to the left or right than the original, who's to know? Nature gives us so many wonderful variations in one flower that any number of drawings of that flower will look pleasing. Now that you know this secret, I hope you will feel confident drawing and painting your own botanicals as well as the projects in this book.

Like decorative painting, drawing can also be broken down into a step-by-step approach. Following these steps will help you to achieve a flower drawing that you will be proud of.

STEP 1: CHOOSE YOUR SUBJECT AND FIND REFERENCE MATERIAL

Flower shapes range from the simple to the complex. If you are just learning to draw, or you want to build your confidence, begin with a simple flower such as a daisy. A daisy has one main flower with a straightforward arrangement of petals. A more complex flower, such as a rose or lilac, may have many flowers with multiple layers of petals. You could also try a pansy, sunflower, coneflower, bluebell or impatiens.

With time and practice the six steps outlined in this chapter will become second nature to you and you will no longer view flowers as hard or easy; you will just see them as different subjects to draw.

If you have some drawing experience, you may want to try a daffodil, tulip, wild rose, hybrid tea rose, poppy, fuchsia, lily or zinnia.

If you have more experience and want to challenge yourself, try the flowers with more complex structures,

This front view black-eyed Susan is a simple flower, perfect for beginners. Its construction is the same as a daisy's.

See how this cabbage rose is more complex, with its multiple layers of petals?

such as a cabbage rose, peony, carnation, chrysanthemum, lilac, hyacinth, hydrangea, iris or gladiolus.

Now begin to look for reference material. The best reference material for a botanical drawing is a live flower. Drawing from life allows you to view the subject from all angles and allows you to see the actual coloring, complete with its variations throughout the flower, stem and leaf.

If you work from a live sample, you will have to work more quickly than if you work from a photograph. As the flower ages, its posture and color will change. To help prolong the life of the flower, place it in water or water-soaked floral foam.

Sometimes, however, it is not possible to work from a live sample. For example, it can be impossible to find lilacs in January or poinsettias in July, even at a professional florist shop. Photographic reference then becomes essential to your drawing. If you plan on drawing flowers on a regular basis, it is very helpful to maintain photographic reference files with one flower type per file. Clip flower photos from gardening and decorating magazines, seed catalogs, nursery advertisements, etc.

The best reference photographs are those you take yourself because you can photograph the flowers with your drawings in mind. Always keep your camera loaded with film and shoot photos on a regular basis as flowers come in and out of season.

Shoot the flower from all angles including from the sides, top and back. This variety can really add interest to your final drawing. Also remember to photograph the flower in varying levels of bloom. Photograph the bud stage, the semi-open flower and the flower in full bloom. Photograph the stem and leaves as well.

Finally, shoot the flower from farther away so that the growth habit can be seen. An entire roll of film may be used on one flower type. This is normal and even desirable. The visual information will be invaluable when drawing your floral botanicals, and if your photos are clear enough and plentiful enough, it can be as good as working from life.

Here are some of my photo references. They include clippings from seed catalogs, magazines and books, and reference photos I have taken.

Take close up pictures showing each flower at different angles and different stages of bloom.

Also shoot the flower from a distance to show growth habit of the leaves and stem.

STEP 2: CLOSELY OBSERVE DEFINING CHARACTERISTICS

This is the most important step. Place your floral sample in front of you, or if working from photographs, spread these out on your work surface. Look at your reference material in an analytical way. First, determine the most distinguishing characteristics of your flower. For a rose it may be the multi-petaled structure, for a pansy it may be the striking coloring, for a lupine it may be the tall and spiky shape. These are the characteristics that give the flower its own unique look. It will be important that your drawing communicate these characteristics. Continue your analysis in detail. Here are some things that you will want to note.

The Flower

- What is the overall shape of the flower? Is it tall and spiky? Round and full? Tubular? Or perhaps a combination of two or more shapes?
- Does the flower consist of one central bloom or is it made up of many individual florets? How many petals are there in each flower or floret?
- Does the flower have a distinct center? Is the center convex or concave? What is its shape?
- How are the petals attached to the center? Are there pistils and stamens present?
- What is the flower's growth habit? Does it grow straight up or curve at an angle? Is there one main stem with many offshoots, or does each flower grow from its own stem?

The Stem

- Is the stem straight, or does it branch off in spots? Are the off-shooting branches straight, or do they curve? In which direction do they curve?
- Is the stem smooth or bumpy? Is it woody or fibrous? Is it hairy or sleek? Are there thorns?

The Leaves

- How are the leaves shaped? Are they long and bladelike, large and oval, or feathery like a fern?
- What is the texture of the leaf? Is it shiny or dull? Flat or spongy?
- Is the outside edge of the leaf smooth, or is it serrated? Do the serrations come at regular intervals, or are they more random?

- Do the leaves have veins? In what direction do the veins grow? Do they all emanate from a central point, or do they branch off continually from the main vein?

In short, analyze every portion of the flower, stem and leaves and how they are connected to one another. You may find it helpful to take notes as you observe and learn about the flower.

Spending time observing and analyzing your flower will make it easier to draw because you will know exactly what you are trying to communicate in your drawing. Careful observation will also result in a much more realistic drawing.

Study these reference photos. Look at the flowers, stems and leaves and answer the questions on this page to learn to observe the defining characteristics.

STEP 3: DETERMINE THE COMPOSITION

In this step you will work through your first major decision: How will the flower be arranged on the paper? This is known as the composition.

The composition of a botanical drawing is in part determined by the growth habit of the flower. Flowers that grow on long stems with many leaves will lend themselves to a vertical format. Flowers that grow in short, compact groups may suggest a different composition.

To save time and frustration, try several compositions in thumbnail form first. Thumbnails are very small, rough drawings—I find 2" × 4" (5.1cm × 10.2cm) to be a good size. No individual flowers or leaves need to be drawn; just sketch their basic shapes. A rose may be indicated with a circle. A hyacinth might be indicated with a rectangle.

Develop at least three or four thumbnails. View them critically, keeping the points mentioned below in mind. One or two of the sketches will probably stand out to you as being better than the others. These are the ones to choose. If you are unable to make a choice, there are two options: Develop a few more thumbnails and choose from these, or choose one or two thumbnails that you think have the most potential and then do a slightly more detailed sketch from each. At this point, you should find one that is pleasing to you.

Here are some pointers to keep in mind when determining the composition of a botanical illustration.

Balance the Composition
Think of your picture as a seesaw that needs to be in perfect balance. If an imaginary line were placed down the center of the drawing, would the seesaw balance? Use the same test to check the composition horizontally.

Balance does not mean that identical elements or the same number of elements must be placed on either side of the imaginary center. It means that the elements must be of equal visual weight. For example, two large flowers might be balanced on the opposite side of the drawing with three small flowers or two small flowers and a leaf. Flowers in the top half of the drawing can be balanced in the lower half of the composition with additional flowers or the stem and leaves.

Simplify
It is not necessary, or even desirable, to draw every leaf and floret. In fact, drawing every single flower, bud or leaf that you see can result in a very crowded and confusing drawing. Edit what you see and capture just a few of the most representative flowers and leaves.

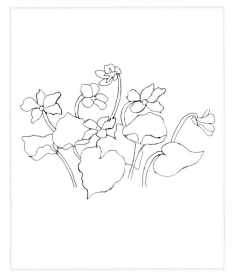

Shorter, compact flowers may work better in a horizontal or oval format. These two sketches are called thumbnail sketches.

Flowers with long stems and upright leaves look best in a vertical format.

Notice how the leaves and flowers on the right of this sketch are balanced by four different elements on the left.

Here the flowers on top are balanced by the leaves in the lower half of the composition.

Add Visual Variety and Movement

Use more than one view of the flower and leaves. A drawing that only shows flowers and leaves facing forward is flat and uninteresting. Include various side views as well. Also include the flower at various points of flowering, from the bud stage to partially open to fully open. The backs of flowers can also add interest and variety to the drawing.

Position some leaves and flowers in front of others. This will create depth and realism.

Include movement in your composition. Flowers drawn straight and upright appear lifeless and stiff. Add some curve to the stem based on the flower's natural growth habit. This will add fluidity and grace to your drawing, as well as interest.

Plan Ahead

Please don't cut off the flowers' heads! Beginning students frequently find themselves running out of room on the page. Flowers end up headless or without adequate-length stems. This problem can be easily avoided by planning the composition before beginning the drawing.

WRONG

This composition contains too many details. It looks crowded and confusing.

BETTER

By editing the composition you can capture the main flowers and leaves, creating better balance and a more pleasing design.

WRONG

Notice how flat this sketch looks with all the elements facing forward.

BETTER

Showing some flowers and leaves and different angles adds interest.

WRONG

These flowers are too straight and stiff.

BETTER

These flowers overlap each other in places and the stems curve as they do in nature.

Step 4: Block in Shapes

What size would you like your finished drawing to be? If you plan to frame your work, it is helpful to choose dimensions that will fit standard frame sizes such as 5" × 7" (12.7cm × 17.8cm), 8" × 10" (20.3cm × 25.4cm), 11" × 14" (27.9cm × 35.6cm), etc. By using a standard size, you will be able to purchase a precut mat and frame (see chapter 5). This will be much less expensive than having your drawing custom matted and framed.

It is important to note that the inside dimensions of precut mats are usually ½-inch (1.3cm) smaller than the standard frame size. For example, a mat precut to fit an 8" × 10" (20.3cm × 25.4cm) picture is usually cut to 7½" × 9½" (19.1cm × 24.1cm).

When you have determined the desired size of your finished drawing, draw a rectangle, square, oval, etc., of the desired size of your finished drawing onto tracing paper. Leave an additional 2-inch (5.1cm) margin all around to allow for wear and tear on the tracing paper.

As you block in your shapes, do not spend time developing or adding details to any one flower or leaf. You may find that things need to be moved once you have blocked in the rest of the elements. The temptation to add detail too early is great. Ed Seltzer, my inspirational art school drawing instructor, threatened to take all of our pencils away from us and replace them with children's jumbo crayons. This, he told us, would force us to stay away from the detail until the composition was finalized. Good advice. You may want to try it yourself if you find yourself straying into detail too soon.

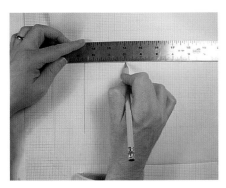

1 To draw this shape accurately, slip a piece of graph paper under your tracing paper and use these lines and a ruler to draw in the desired dimensions. This works best for drawings that will be placed in a square or rectangular mat or frame.

Or, purchase the mat and/or frame that you plan to use and trace its inside dimensions onto the tracing paper. This is particularly helpful for drawings that will be placed in an oval or round mat. These shapes can be tricky to draw accurately.

2 Begin to block in the drawing by indicating a few main reference points on your tracing paper. Mark where the topmost flower or leaf will fall, where the stem will begin and end and where the main flowers and leaves will be placed. This will ensure that the composition will be correctly proportioned on the page with enough room for all elements.

3 Now refer to your thumbnail sketch and live flower or photographs and begin to draw in the basic shapes of your composition. Use simple shapes to indicate where each flower, stem and leaf will be placed.

4 If you wish to change an element, try out the change before erasing by drawing the proposed new elements on a separate sheet of tracing paper and laying the drawing over the original.

Once you have blocked in your drawing, assess how it looks as a whole. Is it balanced? Is there enough variety in the elements? Is it too crowded or too sparse in any one place? In short, does it please you?

You may wish to change the angle, size or profile of certain leaves or flowers. However, you may not want to erase what you have completed in the event that you choose to use this first version. One of the advantages of working on tracing paper is the ability to easily test alternate compositions. Simply draw the proposed new elements on a separate sheet of tracing paper and overlay this drawing onto the original. The translucency of the tracing paper will allow you to view both options and choose the one that looks best.

STEP 5: REFINE SHAPES

Starting at the top left-hand corner of the composition if you are right-handed, or the top right corner if you are left-handed, begin to refine each element of the drawing. While you work, place a sheet of blank tracing paper over the bottom section of drawing. This will keep your drawing surface clean and free of smudges.

As you refine each element, refer frequently to your reference material and your original observation notes from step 1.

Refining the Flowers

Start with the center, or the most prominent petal if the flower has no center. Begin to add the petals. Check their sizes and proportions against the reference material. Are the petals all the same size, or are some larger or smaller? Are the petals in correct proportion to the rest of the flower? As you draw, continually check the accu-

Breaking a Flower Into Basic Shapes

You will find that nature plays favorites. The same shapes appear repeatedly throughout the flower world. Common shapes are dinner plates (daisy, aster, zinnia), cones (lupine, foxglove, red hot poker), cups (poppy, hybrid tea rose, tulip), spheres (cabbage rose, peony, hydrangea) and rectangles or tubes (liatris, hyacinth). Some flowers have compound structures and are composed of more than one shape. For example, a daffodil is a tube on petals that form a dinner plate shape. Once you identify the main shape or shapes, it will be easier to block in the drawing.

DINNER PLATE   CONE   CUP

SPHERE   RECTANGLE OR TUBE

This daffodil is made up of two basic shapes: a tube and a dinner plate.

racy of your drawing against your live sample or photograph. It is helpful to block in the overall outline and check the size and shape before refining each petal.

Adding the Stems

When attaching the stem to a flower, make sure that it connects directly to the flower head. A common mistake is to connect the stem to the flower at a random point. This will result in inaccurate and odd-looking flower portraits.

Note how the stem is attached to the flower head. At the point of connection the stem usually becomes wider. If this area is drawn too narrowly, it will appear that the stem cannot support the weight of the flower. Similarly, when stems branch off and form secondary stems, the connecting point is also wider to support the weight of the new branch.

Adding the Leaves

Showing leaves from differing angles adds vitality to the drawing. For example, several turned leaves will add points of interest. The backs of leaves are often a different value than the fronts, and this will add drama as well. Some artists also like to add the effects of nature by showing bug bites or torn edges. Using some of these special treatments will enhance your drawing, but use them sparingly for the best effect.

The most common error made when adding leaves is to draw a generic leaf shape instead of the leaf actually on the flower. Leaves vary as much as flowers in size, shape and texture, but often they are all portrayed as a generic oval shape.

Compare the blade-shaped leaves of the iris to the heart-shaped leaves of the lilac to the lacy leaves of a cosmos. What tremendous variety!

Spend as much time drawing the leaves as the flowers. The effort will be well rewarded with a more accurate, interesting and realistic drawing.

End With the Details

Now add the finishing touches. Add serrations and veins to the leaves and pistils and stamens to the flowers, if applicable. Add any distinguishing characteristics of the flower, such as the spots on a tiger lily or the hair on a zinnia stem. It is also traditional to add the name of the flower, in Latin or English, near the bottom portion of the flower.

WRONG

When refining the stem, don't connect it to the flower at a random point, as on the left flower. The stem on the right is too narrow at the point of connection and looks like it may break.

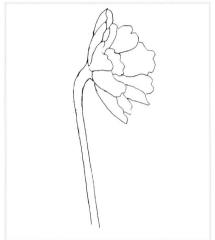

BETTER

The stem should connect directly to the flower head. See how the stem in this illustration widens as it connects to the flower?

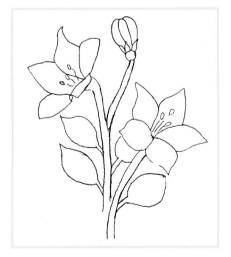

WRONG

These leaves are all facing in one direction and are generic in shape.

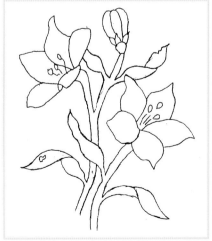

BETTER

Here the correct leaf shape has been used. I've also turned some of the leaves and added a few bug bites and torn edges for interest.

STEP 6: CREATE DEPTH AND REALISM WITH VALUES

This step creates depth in the drawing by adding highlights and shading. To create depth a minimum of three values are needed: light, medium and dark. More depth can be created with five values: very light, light, medium, dark and very dark.

First, determine the direction of the light source. If you are working from a live specimen, you can arrange for the light source to come from any direction desired by placing a lamp in the preferred location.

If you are working from photographs, this can be tricky as the light source may vary from photo to photo. In this case, arbitrarily assign a light source in your own mind, ignoring the highlights and shadows in the photos when they contradict your chosen source.

A common and effective placement is to have the light coming in from either the upper left-hand or right-hand corner of the drawing. The direction you choose is not important. What is important is that the source remains completely consistent throughout the drawing. Consistency will bring the drawing to life and add depth.

Light values are the highlights. The darker values are the shading. The middle value works as the transition between the light and the dark. The lightest values will fall directly where the light source hits the object. It may help to think of the light source as the sun. Things are always lightest and brightest directly where the sun hits.

The darkest values will fall farthest away from the light source or where areas overlap. Frequent areas of darkest value include where petals are joined to the center, the area where the stem meets the flower and the area of petals and leaves that dip down away from the light source.

Do not skip values. Never move from areas of dark to light, or vice versa, without a middle value as a transition. These transition areas will add a smooth flow to your drawing. Without them the drawing will appear choppy and rough.

When you have completed this step, take a last look at the drawing as a whole. Is the light source consistent? Does the drawing have enough depth? If the drawing appears flat, lighten the highlights and darken the shadings to create more contrast and therefore more depth.

Use Value to "Move" Elements

Elements can be pulled forward by lightening the value; if you wish to push an element farther back, darken the value.

---

dark medium light

You need at least three values to create depth.

very dark dark medium light very light

With five values you can create better depth.

The lightest values are the highlights. They fall directly where the sun hits.

The medium value is the transition between light and dark.

The darkest values fall farthest away from the light source or where areas overlap.

Trouble Shooting

At times, you may become stuck. No matter what you put down on paper it just looks wrong. There are several things that you can do to find your mistake.

1. TRY NEW OPTIONS WITH A TRACING PAPER OVERLAY

Redraw the troublesome element onto a separate sheet of tracing paper, mask out the original element with a piece of white paper and overlay this drawing on the original. Changing the size or orientation of the element may help with the problem.

2. CHECK PROPORTIONS

Using your reference material or live specimen, carefully observe the flower or leaf that you are trying to draw. Note its height versus its width, and verbalize its proportions to yourself. For example, "In general, the leaves seem to be twice as long as they are wide." Then check your drawing. Have you portrayed these proportions accurately? If not, adjust your drawing.

3. CHECK THE RELATIVE ANGLES

At times we may see a leaf or petal as more upright or angled than it actually is. Unfortunately, if the angle of one petal or leaf is off, all the subsequent petals and leaves will be off as well. To check your angles, hold a straightedge up to the element in question in your reference material.

A ruler can be used or, more conveniently, your finger. Judge the angle of the petal or leaf against the straightedge. Is it angled more or less than your original perception? Adjust your drawing by what is actually shown in your reference material as opposed to casual observation.

4. CHECK PERSPECTIVE AND FORESHORTENING

Perspective states that objects appear larger the closer they are to you. As an object moves away from you, it appears smaller. Perspective, along with light and shade, create depth in a drawing. As you draw and check your work, keep in mind that as a flower or leaf comes closer to the viewer it appears larger and as it recedes it appears smaller.

When the perspective is severe and the object comes at the viewer at a close and sharp angle, it is called foreshortening. When drawing a foreshortened flower or leaf, draw exactly what you see on your reference material no matter how odd the shape may look. You'll be surprised at how accurate the drawing will look. It can also be helpful to temporarily turn your drawing and reference upside down as you draw. This helps your eye to stop making assumptions that then translate to your hand.

For detailed instruction on perspective and foreshortening, visit your local library or bookstore. There are many well-written and illustrated art books that focus exclusively on perspective and foreshortening.

5. GET A FRESH PERSPECTIVE

Ask for help. Drawing doesn't need to be a solo pursuit. Sometimes you may have been working so closely on a drawing that you can no longer see it objectively. Ask a spouse, co-worker or friend for an opinion. Someone else's fresh eyes may see what is wrong at first glance.

Another trick is to view the drawing in a mirror. Sometimes this new orientation will make errors easier to spot.

Often the mistake will be found using just one of these options. At times the error is a combination of several errors. By working through the options, you will discover the inconsistencies and be able to correct them accordingly.

CHAPTER 4

Painting & Finishing Techniques

I painted all of the projects in this book with one of the three highlighting and shading techniques demonstrated in this chapter: water blended, brush blended or unblended. The Bleeding Heart and Wild Roses projects were painted with a water-blended technique, which creates a very soft, old-fashioned look. The Spring Bulbs project and the Herb & Wildflower Garden Samplers were painted with an unblended technique. The remaining projects were painted with a brush-blended wet-on-wet technique.

LAYING A WASH AND THE WATER-BLENDED TECHNIQUE

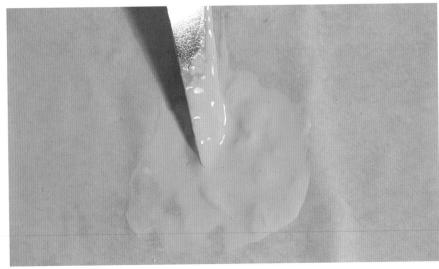

1 **Laying a Wash**

On a prepared Masterson Sta-Wet Palette, mix one part paint to two parts water using the Loew-Cornell no. 609 palette knife. The thinned paint mix will create the transparent look characteristic of washes.

dry border

2 Moisten the section you wish to wash with clean water, leaving an ⅛-inch (0.3cm) border inside the edges dry. This will prevent the paint from bleeding outside the edges.

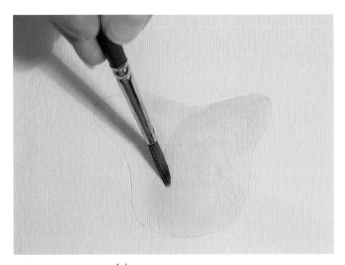

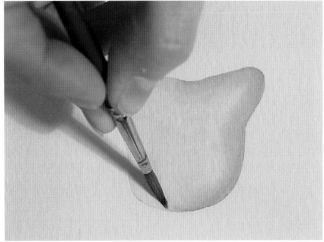

3 | *Fading to White*

Load a brush with the thinned paint and blot the excess on a dry paper towel. Begin painting along the inside edge of the area. The moistened paper will carry the paint through the section. If the instructions do not call for first laying in a wash, the shading color will blend into the white of the paper; this is also referred to as "fading to white."

4 | *Water-Blended Technique*

Thin the color you wish to blend into the first color as instructed in step 1. After the initial wash has dried completely, re-wet the section as instructed in step 2. Lay in the second color as instructed in step 3. Repeat as needed.

THE BRUSH-BLENDED WET-ON-WET TECHNIQUE

This technique looks great and it's much quicker than the traditional floating technique often used in decorative painting. It does take a little practice to master, but you will be rewarded with a beautiful piece.

1 | Place the colors you wish to blend on a prepared Masterson Sta-Wet Palette. Do not add any additional water to the paint. Load a brush approximately three-fourths of the way down the hairs.

2 | Basecoat the section being painted with the light- or mid-value color, as indicated in the project. Allow this color to dry until it reaches a tacky stage (about 75% dry). Add the next value indicated. At the point where the values meet, blend by softly moving the brush across the two values. A light touch is necessary to avoid lifting the paint and leaving a hole. If additional values are needed, once again allow the paint to dry to a tacky stage before adding the next color.

UNBLENDED SHADING AND HIGHLIGHTING

Unblended shading and highlighting are quick and easy techniques. You will love the immediacy of the results.

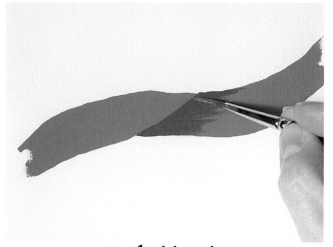

Unblended Shading

Load the brush with a medium amount of paint. Start at the edge of the object being shaded and paint in very closely spaced parallel lines.

Unblended Highlighting

Load the brush with a medium amount of paint. Start at the edge of the object being highlighted and paint in very closely spaced parallel lines.

INTENSIFYING UNBLENDED SHADING AND HIGHLIGHTING

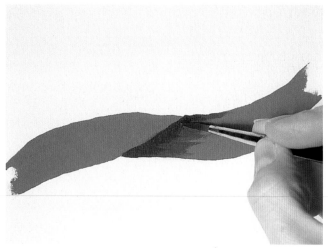

Intensifying Shading

Use the same procedure as for unblended shading with a paint color one value darker. Cover only approximately two-thirds of the first shading with these parallel lines.

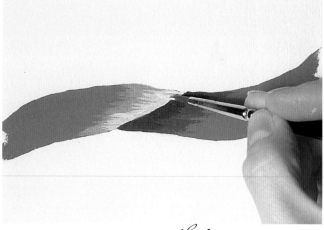

Intensifying Highlighting

Use the same procedure as for unblended highlighting with a paint color one value lighter. Cover only approximately two-thirds of the first highlighting with these parallel lines.

WET-ON-WET SHADING AND HIGHLIGHTING

Shading

Load the brush with a medium amount of paint and apply the basecoat (see page 31). While the basecoat is still wet, work from the inside edge of the area to paint in the shading color. Brush blend the two colors together at the point where the shading ends.

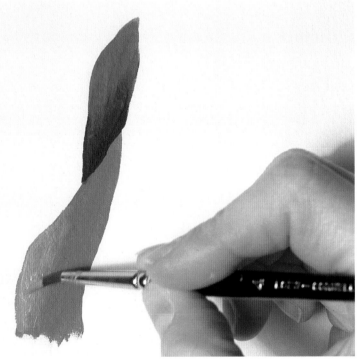

Highlighting

Load the brush with a medium amount of paint and apply the basecoat (see page 31). While the basecoat is still wet, work from the inside edge of the area to paint in the highlighting color. Brush blend the two colors together at the point where the highlighting ends.

Intensifying Wet-on-Wet Shading and Highlighting

Intensifying Shading

While the shading color is still wet, work from the inside edge of the area to paint in the next value darker shading color. Cover approximately two-thirds of the first shading.

Intensifying Highlighting

While the highlighting color is still wet, work from the inside edge of the area to paint in the next value lighter highlighting color. Cover approximately two-thirds of the first highlight.

Choppy Shading

Basecoat the area (see page 31). While the basecoat is still wet, work from the inside edge of the area to paint in the shading color. Brush blend the two colors, but allow brushstrokes to show. Do not blend until smooth.

BASECOATING

Load the brush with a medium amount of paint. Begin to basecoat an area by starting on any outside edge. Place the tip of the brush just inside of the pattern line, and move the brush along the pattern line. This will create a crisp edge. Continue to pull paint down into the object being basecoated until the surface is covered. Work small sections at a time.

DRYBRUSHING

Drybrushing is a quick and effective way to add dazzling highlights to any piece of artwork.

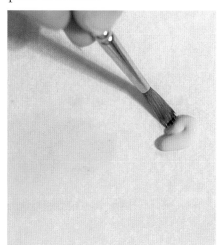

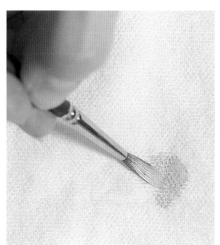

1 Place paint on a prepared palette. Do not add any additional water. Wet a brush and blot thoroughly on a dry paper towel. Spread the bristles flat and load as shown.

2 Wipe off the excess paint on a dry paper towel.

3 Lightly move the brush across the area to be highlighted.

ACCENTING

An accent is a small spot of color that adds life to a painting. Usually, the accent color is taken from the main area of the design, helping to tie the final painting together.

1 | Place paint on a prepared palette. Add a few drops of clean water and mix thoroughly. Moisten a brush and roll into a point on the palette. Load the brush approximately three-fourths of the way up the hairs.

2 | Draw the loaded brush along the area to be accented.

KEEPING BORDERS STRAIGHT

Place paint on a prepared palette. Load a brush with paint thinned with several drops of clean water. Lay the brush down in the middle of the stripe and apply pressure to flatten the bristles. Align the flat edge of the bristles with the edge of the stripe, and move the brush along this edge until it needs to be reloaded. Keeping the brush aligned with the edge will make a straight border with one pass of the brush.

LETTERING

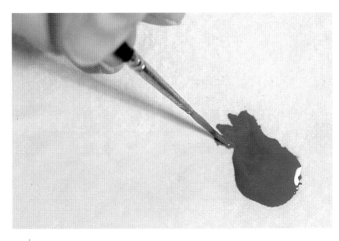

1 | Place paint on a prepared palette. Thin with water until the paint is the consistency of heavy cream. Load a liner brush and twirl the bristles on the palette to achieve a sharp point.

2 | If needed, wipe off any excess paint onto a dry paper towel. Fill in the letters. Use a light touch for better control.

VARNISHING

The wood and metal projects in this book are varnished with Plaid FolkArt Artists' Varnish, matte.

1 | Roll the varnish bottle gently on a tabletop. Do not shake. A gentle rolling will prevent air bubbles from forming, which can be transferred to the surface and mar the finish.

2 | Gently pour a small amount of varnish onto a glass or china plate. Load a Loew-Cornell series 790 1-inch (25mm) oval wash brush with varnish. The oval shape of this brush will help to prevent unsightly ridges from forming on the surface.

3 | Stroke the loaded brush softly across the surface in thin layers. For a smooth finish, do not rework the varnish as it is drying. Allow each coat to dry thoroughly before adding the next. For maximum protection, varnish with at least three coats.

Matting & Framing Artwork

USING STANDARD SIZES

Professional custom matting and framing of artwork can be very expensive, but there is no denying the finish and beauty it adds to any picture. Your artwork will always be greatly enhanced by the addition of a carefully chosen mat and frame. This chapter outlines how to save substantial amounts of money by doing the matting and framing on your own.

It is much easier and less expensive to mat and frame artwork when it fits standard mat and frame sizes, such as 4" × 6" (10.2cm × 15.2cm), 5" × 7" (12.7cm × 17.8cm), 8" × 10" (20.3cm × 25.4cm), 11" × 14" (27.9cm × 35.6cm), etc. Stock mats and frames are available in standard sizes at reasonable prices.

If the artwork is a nonstandard size, more expensive custom framing may be necessary.

All projects in this book were specially designed to fit standard-size mats and frames. If you design your own original floral botanicals, keep standard sizes in mind and you will be able to easily frame your own work.

MATERIALS

There are times when it is acceptable, and sometimes even preferable, to cut corners to make framing more economical. Buying framing components and doing your own framing is a good opportunity to save money. Buying inferior materials is not.

Make sure that all materials that will touch the artwork—the mat, the tape used to affix the artwork to the mat and the backing—are of archival quality and acid free. If an item is acid free, it will generally say so on the packaging. Products that are not acid free will cause the artwork to turn brown and brittle over time. This damage cannot be repaired.

MATS

Mats not only greatly enhance a framed piece, they offer protection as well. They provide rigidity and support to the artwork and also provide an important separation between the artwork and the glass, protecting the art from damage should humidity develop inside the framed piece.

PRECUT MATS

Standard-size, precut mats may be purchased at art and craft supply stores. The benefit to using precut mats is that the mat is already cut for you. The drawback is that precut mats are available in a very limited color range.

CUSTOM MATS

Stores with a framing department will have a larger selection of mats in their custom framing area where the mat selected can be cut to size. This will cost more than a stock mat but still be within a reasonable cost.

CUTTING YOUR OWN MATS

Another option is to purchase a mat cutter and cut your own mats. If you plan to paint and frame several projects and other pieces of artwork or memorabilia, it is worth investing in a mat cutter.

Cutting your own mats saves expense in the long run, especially when choosing options such as double and triple mats or multiple openings that become very pricey if purchased at retail.

Cutting your own mats also gives you the option of making other high-end custom cuts such as irregular corners, arches, etc.

A mat cutting system may be purchased at most art supply stores. The systems I find the most flexible and easy to use are Alto's 4501 Mat Cutting System and 4505 Deluxe Mat Cutting System. Alto's systems are flexible and accurate, allow unlimited options for customization and have lifetime warranties. They are also one of the few systems that may be used by both right- and left-handers.

Uncut mat board may be purchased at art and frame supply shops. The Crescent Cardboard Company, whose mats were used in this book, produces many acid-free mat boards.

FRAMES

Frame prices can vary wildly. There are frames on the market that are a work of art by themselves. These are wonderful to use and add a luxurious finish to the piece. If you are on a budget, however, there are several options that result in pieces that look just as handsome.

Discount stores often sell frames at low prices. However, be sure to discard any mat and backing that came with the frame. When the frame is very inexpensive, the mat and backing materials are probably not acid free. Replace them with archival, acid-free material. Often the frame can be repainted with acrylic paints if the color is not to your liking.

Other good sources for frames are garage sales and flea markets. Don't pass up those ugly, two dollar pictures until you have looked at the frames. If they are in relatively good condition, they can easily be repainted.

Embellishments can also be added for a custom look. Walnut Hollow offers hobby wood in many shapes, patterns and sizes that enhance any frame.

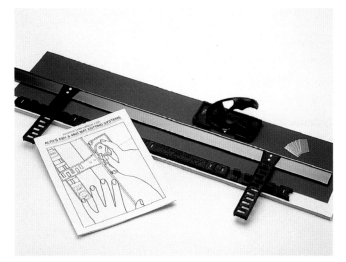

Alto's Mat Cutting System

You can repaint inexpensive or outdated frames to make them more attractive.

Here I've added Walnut Hollow hobby wood embellishments to my repainted frame.

ADHESIVES

Tape is commonly used to attach the artwork to the mat or backing. Do not use the cellophane tape that is used to wrap gifts; it is full of acid. The staining, brown residue that appears when the tape ages will damage your artwork irreparably.

The projects in this book were attached to their mats with Keep A Memory Acid Free Mounting Adhesive by Therm O Web. This product can be purchased at craft, scrapbooking and art supply stores.

BACKING

Discard the cardboard backing that comes with most frames. Replace it with white, acid-free mat board or museum board. This is more expensive than scrap cardboard, but the backing comes into contact with the entire piece of artwork; therefore, it should be acid free to protect the work.

GLASS

If your frame did not come with glass, check your yellow pages for a local glass dealer. Most carry picture glass and will cut it to size for you. A piece of 11" × 14" (27.9cm × 35.6cm) picture glass should cost under ten dollars. Larger sizes will cost more.

Be sure to bring the frame with you when you go to have the glass cut. Even small variations from the standard will affect the fit of the glass. Also bring a blanket or padding to protect the glass on the way home. Most glass shops do not provide packing material.

AN INEXPENSIVE AND EASY WAY TO FRAME ARTWORK

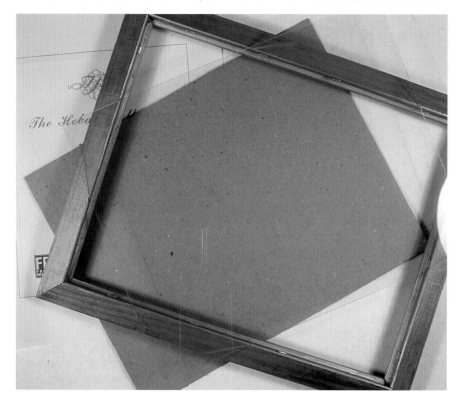

1 Disassemble the frame and its components. Clean both sides of the glass with glass or window cleaner and dry thoroughly.

2 Wash and dry your hands before touching the artwork. Position the cut mat on top of the artwork and secure the artwork to it temporarily with low-tack tape.

3 | Turn the artwork and mat over. Affix the artwork to the mat with Therm O Web Keep A Memory Acid Free Mounting Adhesive. This product is double sided, so it will be easy to keep the artwork aligned. Remove the temporarily affixed low-tack tape.

4 | Place the glass back into the frame. Position the artwork and mat face down onto the glass.

5 | Lay the acid-free backing on top of the matted artwork. Secure the backing into the frame with any hardware that came with the frame. Sealing the perimeter with an acid-free tape will provide additional dust protection.

Bleeding Hearts

It's a pity that such a beautiful flower has such a sad name. However, it is easy to see why the name has continued through the years: The rosy red, heart-shaped flowers are combined with a blood-drop-shaped throat. If you prefer, you can use this flower's less common name, lady's locket. The bleeding heart is an ideal botanical subject. The naturally complementary color combination of red and green is striking; its long, arching stem contributes to a graceful composition; and the delicate attachment of the flower to the stem results in flower hearts that look like they will dance even in the slightest breeze.

Plaid FolkArt Acrylic Paints

Burgundy	Magenta	Spring Rose
Old Ivy	Grass Green	Lime Yellow
Gray Green	French Vanilla	

Materials continued on page 40.

This pattern may be hand-traced or photocopied for personal use only. Enlarge on a photocopier at 132% to return to full size.

© 2000 Michelle Temares

Bleeding Heart

Materials, continued

SURFACE

❧ 10" × 14" (25.4cm × 35.6cm) piece of Winsor & Newton 140-lb. (300gsm) cold-press watercolor paper

BRUSHES

❧ Loew-Cornell Art Tec no. 4 sable
❧ Loew-Cornell series 7350, no. 2 liner

ADDITIONAL SUPPLIES

❧ Masterson Sta-Wet Palette
❧ transferring supplies
❧ Krylon Workable Fixative, no. 1306
❧ 11" × 14" (27.9cm × 35.6cm) frame

❧ 11" × 14" (27.9cm × 35.6cm) mat with 7½" × 9½" (19.1cm × 22.9cm) opening
❧ Therm O Web Keep A Memory Acid Free Mounting Adhesive

Use the no. 4 sable for all of the following steps, except the lettering.

1 | Lightly moisten the leaves and stems with water and then basecoat with Lime Yellow.

2 | While the basecoat is still wet, shade the outer edges of the stems and leaves and along the leaf veins with Grass Green.

3 | Deepen the shading with Old Ivy.

4 | Accent the darkest areas of the stems and leaves with Burgundy to deepen the shading one additional value. The darkest areas are where the stems join leaves and flowers, and along the vein lines in the leaves.

5 | Lightly moisten the flowers with water. Basecoat the main portion of the flowers with Spring Rose and the throats with French Vanilla.

6 | While the basecoat is still wet, shade the main portion of the flowers with Magenta. Leave the Spring Rose basecoat showing in the centers of the flowers as a highlight.

7 | Repeat with Burgundy to deepen the shading.

8 | Accent the darkest areas of the flowers with Old Ivy to deepen the shading one additional value. The darkest areas are at the edges of the flowers and where the flowers join the stems.

9 | Shade the throat of the flowers with Gray Green.

10 | Deepen some Burgundy with a touch of Old Ivy and thin to an inky consistency. Use this color to paint the outer border. Paint the inner border with thinned Gray Green.

11 | Paint in the lettering with thinned Burgundy on the no. 2 liner brush.

Bleeding Heart

12 | When the painting is thoroughly dry, spray it lightly with Krylon Workable Fixative to protect it against water damage and dirt.

Wild Roses

Poems abound with mentions of it, artists have captured it, and romance would be nowhere without it—the rose is high on everyone's list of favorite flowers. Throughout history it has been a popular painting subject for the artist and an equally loved subject of the viewer.

The variety of roses available is staggering; there are cabbage roses, tea roses and hybrid roses, just to name a few.

The roses in this project are old-fashioned wild roses. Their smell is heavenly, and with consistent pruning they will grace your garden with blooms at least twice during the growing season.

I did these paintings in two coordinating warm color schemes. If you prefer one coloring over the other, don't hesitate to paint both designs with the same colors. Either way, they make a lovely grouping on any wall.

Plaid FolkArt Acrylic Paints

For the yellow & orange roses			
Lipstick Red	Glazed Carrots	Yellow Ochre (Artists' Pigment)	Lemon Custard
Lemonade	Hauser Green Medium (Artists' Pigment)	Hauser Green Light (Artists' Pigment)	Lime Yellow

For the pink & red roses			
Fuchsia	Light Fuchsia	Bright Baby Pink	Hauser Green Medium (Artists' Pigment)
Hauser Green Light (Artists' Pigment)	Yellow Ochre (Artists' Pigment)	Lemonade	

Materials continued on page 48.

PATTERN FOR YELLOW & ORANGE ROSES

Wild Rose

© 2000 Michelle Temares

The patterns on pages 46–47 may be hand-traced or photocopied for personal use only. Enlarge at 107% to bring them up to full size.

Wild Rose

© 2000 Michelle Temares

PAINTING THE YELLOW & ORANGE ROSES

Use the no. 4 sable for all of the following steps, except where another brush is indicated.

Materials, continued

SURFACE
❦ 10" × 14" (25.4cm × 35.6cm) piece of Winsor & Newton 140-lb. (300gsm) cold-press watercolor paper for each design

BRUSHES
❦ Loew-Cornell Art Tec no. 4 sable
❦ Loew-Cornell series 7350, no. 2 liner
❦ Loew-Cornell series 7450, no. 2 flat

ADDITIONAL SUPPLIES
❦ Masterson Sta-Wet Palette
❦ transferring supplies
❦ Krylon Workable Fixative, no. 1306
❦ two 11" × 14" (27.9cm × 35.6cm) mats with 7½" × 9½" (19.1cm × 22.9cm) oval opening
❦ two 11" × 14" (27.9cm × 35.6cm) frames
❦ Therm O Web Keep A Memory Acid Free Mounting Adhesive

1 | Wash over the flower petals with Lemonade, allowing the color to fade to white toward the flower center. Also wash the flower centers with Lemonade. Wash over the leaves with Lime Yellow, allowing the color to fade to white toward the center veins. Also wash the stems with Lime Yellow.

2 | Shade the flowers with Lemon Custard.

3 | Darken the shading with Glazed Carrots.

4 | Shade a final time with Lipstick Red.

5 | Paint in growth lines with the chisel edge of your no. 2 flat brush. Paint in two layers: First paint in the lines with Glazed Carrots and then repeat in the darker portions of the petals with Lipstick Red. The lines should follow the contour of the petals. Bring the growth lines slightly beyond the darker, shaded portion of the petals and into the lighter yellow sections.

6 | Shade inside the rose centers with Hauser Green Light. Shade a little more heavily toward the bottom of the centers. Repeat the shading with Glazed Carrots to soften.

7 | Shade along all leaf veins with Hauser Green Light.

8 | Deepen the shade on the back leaf veins with Hauser Green Medium.

9 | Accent the leaves with Lipstick Red.

10 Dot Yellow Ochre randomly around the flower centers. Add smaller dots in the center of the Yellow Ochre dots with Lemon Custard. Paint in filament lines with Yellow Ochre. Add finer lines of Hauser Green Light on top of the previous lines.

Wild Rose

11 Paint the lettering with the no. 2 liner and a thinned mix of Hauser Green Medium darkened with a touch of Lipstick Red. When the painting is thoroughly dry, spray it lightly with Krylon Workable Fixative to protect it against water damage and dirt.

PAINTING THE PINK & RED ROSES

Use the no. 4 sable for all of the following steps, except where another brush is indicated.

1 | Wash the petals, leaves and stems with Lemonade. Allow the Lemonade to fade to white on the front-most portions of the design.

2 | Shade the flowers with Bright Baby Pink.

3 | Shade the flowers again with Light Fuchsia.

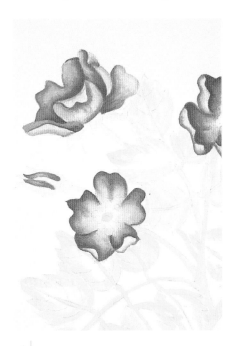

4 | Deepen the shading in the darkest areas with Fuchsia.

5 | Paint in the growth lines with Fuchsia using the chisel edge of the no. 2 flat brush. The lines should follow the contour of the petals. Bring the growth lines slightly beyond the darker, shaded portion of the petals and into the lighter yellow sections.

6 | Dot Yellow Ochre randomly around the flower centers. Randomly add smaller dots of Lemonade to the Yellow Ochre dots.

7 | Paint in the filament lines with Yellow Ochre. Add finer lines of Hauser Green Light on top of the previous lines. Shade inside the rose centers with Hauser Green Light, shading slightly more heavily toward the bottom of the centers. Shade along the stems and leaf veins with Hauser Green Light.

9 | Accent the darkest areas of the leaves with Fuchsia.

8 | Reinforce the shading along the stems and leaf veins with Hauser Green Medium.

Wild Rose

10 | Add the lettering with the no. 2 liner and a thinned mix of Hauser Green Medium darkened with with a touch of Lipstick Red. When the painting is thoroughly dry, spray it lightly with Krylon Workable Fixative to protect it against water damage and dirt.

Spring Bulbs

While the craze for Internet stocks may be a modern phenomenon, speculating in wildly fluctuating investments is not. Flower bulbs, and particularly tulip bulbs, were the Internet investment equivalent in seventeenth-century Holland. At the peak of this period, known as Tulipmania, some individual bulbs were trading for the price of one of Amsterdam's finest homes. The painter in you will be aghast to know that a still life painted by one of Holland's finest painters was less expensive than a fine tulip. Fortunately, you can have your own version of Tulipmania, with the addition of daffodils and hyacinths, at a fraction of the cost and without investment risk.

Plaid FolkArt Acrylic Paints

Rose Pink	Raspberry Sherbet	Mix 1 1 part Wicker White + 1 part Baby Pink	Sweetheart Pink		
Glazed Carrots	Turner's Yellow (Artists' Pigment)	Lemon Custard	Mix 2 1 part Wicker White + 1 part Lemon Custard	Buttercream	Wicker White
Bayberry	Mix 3 1 part Bayberry + 1 part Aspen Green	Mix 4 1 part Wicker White + 1 part Mint Green	Lime Yellow		
Periwinkle	Light Periwinkle	Baby Blue	Mix 5 1 part Wicker White + 1 part Baby Blue		

Materials continued on page 57.

top

center

A

B

A

B

bottom

This pattern may be hand-traced or photocopied for personal use only. Enlarge each of the three pieces at 111% on a photocopier to return to full size.

The pattern pieces for the bowl's sides have been designed to accommodate a slant-sided bowl, which is wider at the top than at the bottom. Transfer each part of the pattern separately, curving the side pieces to fit the bowl and matching the design up at the As and Bs.

The entire piece was painted with the no. 6 ultra round brush, except where indicated in the instructions for the background.

Background

Basecoat the entire bowl with three coats of Wicker White.

Materials, continued

SURFACE

❦ This slanted-side metal bowl is available from Barb Watson's Brushworks
P.O. Box 1467
Moreno, CA 92556
Phone: (909) 653-3780
Web site: www.barbwatson.com

BRUSHES

❦ Loew-Cornell La Corneille series 7400, 1-inch (25mm) rose petal brush
❦ Loew-Cornell series 7020, no. 6 ultra round

ADDITIONAL SUPPLIES

❦ Masterson Sta-Wet Palette
❦ transferring supplies
❦ paper towels
❦ FolkArt Blending Gel
❦ FolkArt Artists' Varnish, matte

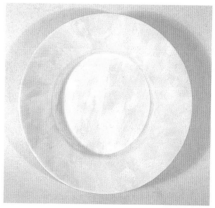

2 | Brush a thin layer of Blending Gel over the entire outside of the bowl. Randomly place brushstrokes of Mix 1, Mix 2, Mix 4 and Mix 5 onto the surface of the bowl.

3 | While still wet, spread the paint by moving the rose petal brush diagonally across the bowl, wiping the brush on a paper towel every few strokes.

4 | Repeat steps 2 and 3 for the inside of the bowl.

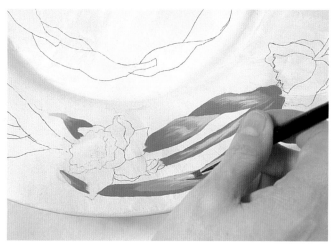

5 | *Daffodil 1*
Basecoat the leaves and stem with Bayberry. Shade with Mix 3.

6 | Highlight the leaves and stem with Lime Yellow.

7 | Basecoat the daffodil with Lemon Custard and shade with Turner's Yellow.

8 | Highlight the daffodil with Buttercream. Paint in the pistils and stamen with Turner's Yellow.

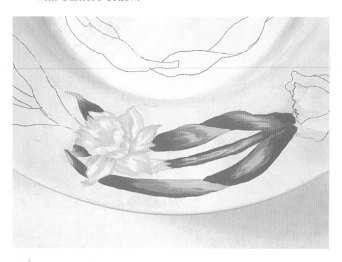

9 | Intensify the shading on the daffodil with Glazed Carrots.

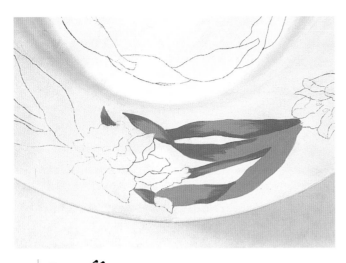

10 | *Daffodil 2*
Basecoat the leaves and stem with Bayberry. Shade with Mix 3.

11 | Highlight the leaves and stem with Lime Yellow.

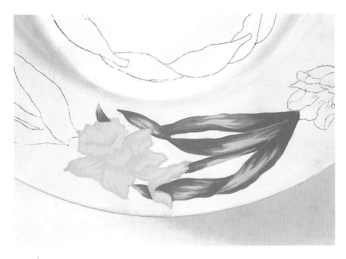

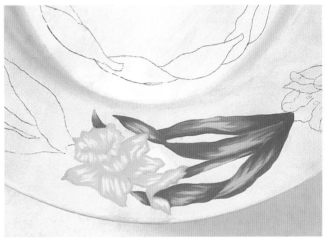

12 | Basecoat the daffodil with Lemon Custard and shade with Turner's Yellow.

13 | Highlight the daffodil with Buttercream. Paint in the pistils and stamen with Turner's Yellow.

14 | Intensify the shading on the daffodil with Glazed Carrots.

15 | *Rear-View Tulip*
Basecoat the main portions of the leaves and stem with Bayberry and the sections where the leaf is turned over with Lime Yellow.

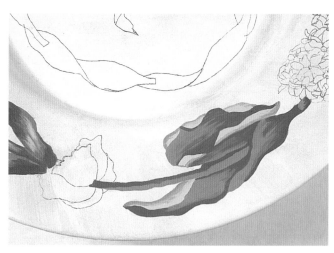

16 | Shade the Bayberry areas with Mix 3 and the Lime Yellow areas with Bayberry.

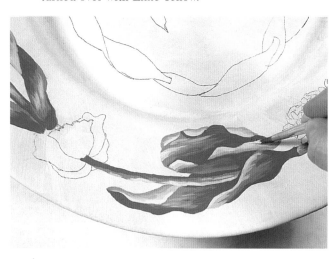

17 | Highlight the Bayberry areas with Lime Yellow and the Lime Yellow areas with Buttercream.

18 | Basecoat the petals with Sweetheart Pink and shade with Rose Pink.

19 | Intensify the shading with Raspberry Sherbet.

20 | Highlight the petals with Lemon Custard and small amounts of Buttercream.

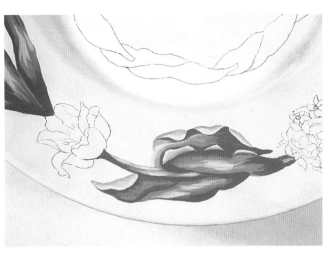

21 | *Open Tulip*
Basecoat the main portions of the leaves and stem with Bayberry and the sections where the leaf is turned over with Lime Yellow. Shade the Bayberry areas with Mix 3 and the Lime Yellow areas with Bayberry.

22 | Highlight the Bayberry areas with Lime Yellow and the Lime Yellow areas with Buttercream.

23 | Basecoat the main petals with Sweetheart Pink and the turned portions with a small amount of Sweetheart Pink.

24 | Shade the main petals with Rose Pink and the turned portions with a small amount of Rose Pink.

25 | Intensify the shading on the main petals with Raspberry Sherbet and on the turned portions with a small amount of Raspberry Sherbet.

26 | Highlight the petals with Lemon Custard and small amounts of Buttercream.

27 *Hyacinth*
Basecoat the leaves and stem with Bayberry and shade with Mix 3.

28 | Highlight with Lime Yellow.

29 | Basecoat the petals with Light Periwinkle and the centers with Periwinkle.

30 | Paint a line of Periwinkle down the center of each petal.

31 | Paint a line of Baby Blue down both sides of each petal.

32 | *Center Motif*
Basecoat the leaves with Bayberry and shade with Mix 3.

33 | Highlight the leaves with Lime Yellow.

34 | Basecoat the tulip with Lemon Custard. Shade with Rose Pink.

35 | Intensify the shading with small amounts of Periwinkle.

36 | Highlight with Buttercream.

37 | *Adding Final Accents*
Accent the daffodils with Periwinkle.

38 | Accent the tulips with Mix 3.

39 | Accent the hyacinths with Glazed Carrots.

40 | Protect the completed bowl with at least three coats of matte varnish.

Morning Glory & Sweet Pea

Morning glories and sweet peas may not be biologically related, but to me they seem to belong together. Both are climbing vines, have beautiful, colorful flowers and bloom throughout the summer. They make a happy marriage when placed side by side in these paintings. These are cheerful projects to paint in the dead of winter when we are so longing for a promise of carefree summer days.

Plaid FolkArt Acrylic Paints

Violet Pansy	Fuchsia	Light Fuchsia	Baby Pink
Periwinkle	Light Periwinkle	Baby Blue	Icy White
Aspen Green	Mystic Green	Mix 1 1 part Lime Yellow + 1 part Mystic Green	Lime Yellow	Lemonade

Materials continued on page 70.

Morning Glory

© 2000 Michelle Temares

The patterns on pages 68–69 may be hand-traced or photocopied for personal use only. Enlarge at 107% to bring them up to full size.

Sweet Pea

Painting the Morning Glories

Paint all of the following steps with the no. 4 sable unless otherwise noted in the instructions.

1 Basecoat the sky area of the border with Light Periwinkle. Dip the deerfoot stippler in Icy White, wipe the excess paint on a paper towel, and randomly pounce into the sky area.

2 Base the veins in the flowers with Icy White. Shade toward either end of each vein with Baby Blue.

3 Base the morning glory centers with Lemonade. Blend Icy White two-thirds of the way to the outside edges of the petals.

Materials, continued

SURFACE
❦ 10" × 12" (25.4cm × 30.5cm) piece of Winsor & Newton 140-lb. (300gsm) cold-press watercolor paper for each design

BRUSHES
❦ Loew-Cornell Art Tec no. 4 sable
❦ Loew-Cornell series 410, ¼-inch (6mm) deerfoot stippler
❦ Loew-Cornell Jackie Shaw no. 2 liner

ADDITIONAL SUPPLIES
❦ Masterson Sta-Wet Palette
❦ transferring supplies
❦ paper towels
❦ Krylon Workable Fixative, no. 1306
❦ two 11" × 14" (27.9cm × 35.6cm) white or off-white mats with 7½" × 9½" (19.1cm × 22.9cm) openings
❦ two 11" × 14" (27.9cm × 35.6cm) frames
❦ Therm O Web Keep A Memory Acid Free Mounting Adhesive

4 | Paint Baby Blue from the edge of the petal until it meets the Icy White. Blend the colors together. Shade into the Baby Blue with Light Periwinkle.

5 | Accent the edges of the petals with a broken line of Periwinkle. Accent the top of the petal veins the same way.

6 | Basecoat the leaves and stems with Lime Yellow and shade with Mix 1. The right sides of the stems and leaves should receive more shading than the left sides.

7 | Deepen the shading with Mystic Green, shading more heavily on the right sides of the leaves and stems.

8 | Place a final shading of Aspen Green in small amounts on the right sides of the leaves and stems.

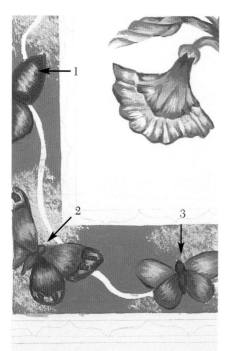

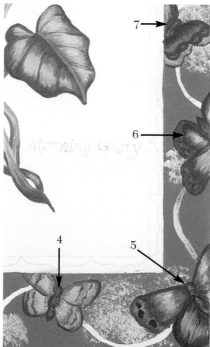

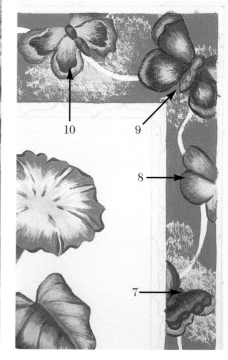

Butterfly 1

Basecoat the upper wings with Lemonade, shade with Violet Pansy and outline with Periwinkle. Basecoat the lower wings with Baby Blue, shade with Periwinkle and outline with Violet Pansy.

Butterfly 2

Basecoat the upper wings with Light Fuchsia, shade with Fuchsia and highlight with Baby Pink. Basecoat the lower wings with Light Fuchsia, shade with Violet Pansy and highlight with Baby Pink. Paint the body and dots with Periwinkle and drybrush with highlights of Light Periwinkle.

Butterfly 3

Basecoat the upper wings with Lime Yellow and shade with Mystic Green. Basecoat the lower wings with Light Fuchsia, shade with Fuchsia and highlight with Baby Pink. Paint the body with Violet Pansy and highlight with Baby Pink. Lightly outline the butterfly with Violet Pansy.

Butterfly 4

Basecoat the stripes with Light Periwinkle and highlight with Baby Blue. Base the wings with Lime Yellow and shade with Mystic Green. Basecoat the body with Periwinkle, highlight with Light Periwinkle and outline with Periwinkle.

Butterfly 5

Basecoat the upper wings with Baby Blue, shade with Fuchsia and highlight with Icy White. Basecoat the lower wings with Lemonade and shade with Violet Pansy. Paint the body with Mystic Green and highlight with Lime Yellow. Basecoat the edge of the upper wing with Baby Blue and shade with Periwinkle, then paint the dots Fuchsia.

Butterfly 6

Basecoat the body with Fuchsia and highlight with Light Fuchsia. Paint the wing border with Fuchsia and paint the dots Periwinkle, highlighting with Light Periwinkle. Basecoat the upper wings (note that this butterfly is upside down) with Lime Yellow and shade with Periwinkle. Basecoat the lower wings with Light Periwinkle, shade with Violet Pansy and highlight with Icy White. Basecoat the body with Periwinkle and highlight with Light Periwinkle. Outline the butterfly with Periwinkle.

Butterfly 7

Basecoat the inner section of the wings with Light Fuchsia, shade with Violet Pansy and highlight with Baby Pink. Basecoat the stripe with Light Periwinkle and shade with Periwinkle. Basecoat the outer edge of the wings with Mix 1 and highlight with Lime Yellow.

Butterfly 8

Basecoat the upper wings with Lemonade, shade with Mystic Green and highlight with Icy White. Basecoat the lower wings with Lemonade, shade with Fuchsia and highlight with Icy White. Outline the butterfly in Violet Pansy.

Butterfly 9

Basecoat the upper wings with Baby Blue, shade with Periwinkle and highlight with Icy White. Basecoat the lower wings with Lemonade and shade with Violet Pansy. Basecoat the body and edging with Mystic Green and shade with Aspen Green. Lightly outline the butterfly with Violet Pansy.

Butterfly 10

Basecoat the body with Periwinkle and highlight with

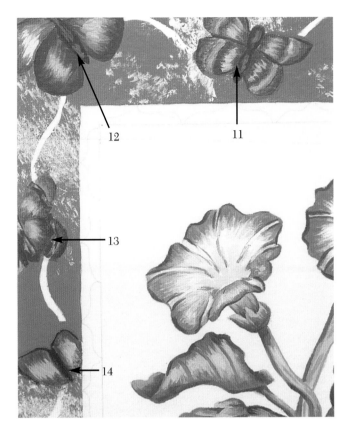

Light Periwinkle. Basecoat the wing borders with Lime Yellow and shade with Aspen Green. Basecoat the upper wings with Baby Blue, shade with Violet Pansy and highlight with Icy White. Basecoat the lower wings with Lime Yellow and shade with Periwinkle.

Butterfly 11

Basecoat the body with Periwinkle and highlight with Light Periwinkle. Basecoat the stripes with Periwinkle and highlight with Baby Blue. Basecoat the upper wings with Light Fuchsia, shade with Fuchsia and highlight with Baby Pink. Basecoat the lower wings with Lime Yellow and shade with Aspen Green.

Butterfly 12

Basecoat the body with Fuchsia and highlight with Light Fuchsia. Basecoat the upper wings with Lemonade and shade with Fuchsia. Basecoat the lower wings with Light Fuchsia, highlight with Baby Pink and shade with Periwinkle.

Butterfly 13

Basecoat the body and stripes with Periwinkle and highlight with Baby Blue. Basecoat the upper wings with Light Fuchsia, shade with Fuchsia and highlight with Icy White. Basecoat the lower wings with Baby Blue and shade with Violet Pansy.

Butterfly 14

Basecoat the upper wings with Lime Yellow, shade with Aspen Green and outline with Violet Pansy.

10 | Basecoat the border ribbon with Mix 1. Shade with Aspen Green.

11 | Highlight the ribbon with Lime Yellow and then add a smaller highlight of Icy White.

12 Paint the narrow inner border Aspen Green and the narrow outer border Light Periwinkle. Basecoat inside the scallops with Icy White and shade with Periwinkle.

13 Basecoat outside the scallops with Lime Yellow and shade with Aspen Green.

14 Paint the lettering with Periwinkle on the no. 2 liner. Paint a thin line of Light Periwinkle along the inside edge of the inner border and Mystic Green along the outside edge of the inner border.

15 Accent the darkest areas of the leaves and stems with Fuchsia.

Morning Glory

16 | Dip the end of the stylus in Aspen Green and press down in the center of each white scallop to create a dot. When the painting is thoroughly dry, spray it lightly with Krylon Workable Fixative to protect it against water damage and dirt. Paint the mat Violet Pansy before framing.

Painting the Sweet Peas

Paint all of the following steps with the no. 4 sable unless otherwise noted in the instructions.

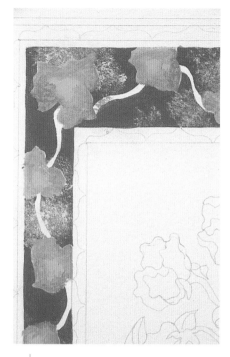

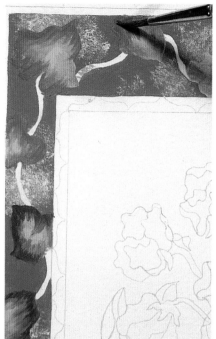

1 | Basecoat the sky with Light Periwinkle. As you did for the morning glories, dip the deerfoot stippler in Icy White, wipe the excess paint on a paper towel and randomly pounce into the border sky area. Basecoat the ivy with Lime Yellow and shade the outer edges with Mix 1.

2 | Shade again with Mystic Green. The shading should look choppy to represent the bumpy texture of the ivy.

3 | Shade a final time with Aspen Green on only one side of each leaf. Add veins with thinned Lime Yellow.

4 | Basecoat the leaves and stems with Lime Yellow and shade with Mix 1. Shade again with Mystic Green. Shade the darkest areas with Aspen Green, as shown in the right picture. The darkest areas are where the stems and leaves intersect, the beginning or end of the stems, along the veins and where the leaves fold.

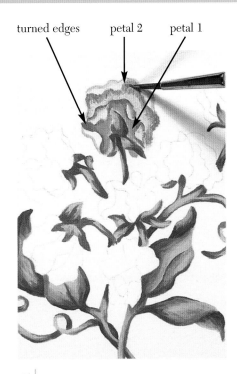

turned edges   petal 2   petal 1

5 | Basecoat all the turned edges of the top sweet pea with Icy White and shade with Baby Blue. Basecoat inside petal 1 with Baby Blue and shade with Light Periwinkle. Basecoat inside petal 2 with Icy White and shade with Light Periwinkle.

6 | With Violet Pansy, shade the top sweet pea a final time and randomly and lightly outline along the edges of the petals.

7 | Basecoat the center sweet pea with Baby Pink. Shade with Light Fuchsia.

8 | Shade the center sweet pea again with Violet Pansy.

9 | Basecoat the upper petals and throat of the bottom center sweet pea with Lemonade. Shade the upper petal with Light Fuchsia. Basecoat the lower petal with Baby Pink and shade with Light Fuchsia.

10 | Shade the bottom center sweet pea again with Fuchsia.

11 Basecoat the top left sweet pea petals with Lemonade and shade with Light Fuchsia. Basecoat the lower left sweet pea petals with Icy White and shade with Baby Blue.

12 Shade the lower left sweet pea again with Light Periwinkle and small amounts of Periwinkle.

13 Basecoat the bud on the right with Baby Pink and shade with Light Fuchsia, then again with Fuchsia. Basecoat the sweet pea below the bud with Lemonade, shade with Light Periwinkle and then with Periwinkle. Add Violet Pansy shading to the top left sweet pea.

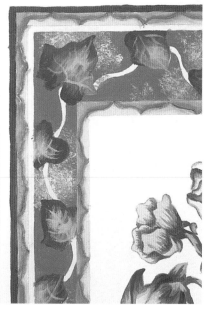

14 Basecoat inside the border scallops with Lemonade and shade with Fuchsia mixed with a touch of Aspen Green. Also paint the narrow outer border with this mix. Basecoat outside the scallops with Baby Blue and shade with Periwinkle.

15 Paint the narrow inner border Aspen Green. Paint a thin line of Light Periwinkle along the inside edge of the inner border and Mystic Green along the outside edge of the inner border. Paint in the lettering with Periwinkle on the no. 2 liner.

16 Dip the end of a stylus in Fuchsia and press in the center of the Lemonade scallops to create dots.

Sweet Pea

17 | Basecoat the ribbon with Mix 1. Shade with Aspen Green. Accent the darkest areas of the leaves and stems with Fuchsia. When the painting is thoroughly dry, spray it lightly with Krylon Workable Fixative to protect it against water damage and dirt. Paint the mat Fuchsia before framing.

Herb & Wildflower

Garden Samplers

These projects make wonderful accent pieces in a kitchen or garden-inspired bedroom or family room. They appear to be antiques, but they are actually painted on new watercolor paper treated with a background technique that creates an aged appearance. It has become popular to achieve this slightly yellowed appearance by using tea or coffee as a dye, but I urge you not to use this method. Over time the acids in the tea and coffee will eat away at the painting, resulting in permanent damage. Safe and durable acrylic paint can achieve the same effects with none of the drawbacks.

Plaid FolkArt Acrylic Paints

Mix 1 5 parts Apple Spice + 1 part Thicket	Apple Spice	Mix 2 5 parts Autumn Leaves + 1 part Heartland Blue	Turner's Yellow (Artists' Pigment)	Country Twill
Thicket	Hauser Green Light (Artists' Pigment)	Lime Yellow		
Heartland Blue	Sterling Blue	Baby Blue		
Purple Passion	Lavender	Purple Lilac	Lavender Sachet	
Rose Pink	Cotton Candy	Wicker White		

Materials continued on page 84.

Nasturtium

Borage

Rosemary

Lavender

Chamomile

Herb Garden

Sage

Chives

Marsh Mallow

© 2000 Michelle Temares

Wild Geranium

Bluebell

Cosmos

Wildflower

Garden

Daisy

Forget Me Not

Wild Lupine

Viola

CREATING A "TEA-STAINED" BACKGROUND

All steps are painted with the no. 4 sable except for the background and lettering. See those steps for the appropriate brush.

Mix approximately 25 parts water to 1 part Country Twill to make a watery wash. Using the 1½-inch (38mm) wash brush, cover the entire surface of the design with this mix. Allow the paper to dry thoroughly before continuing.

Materials, continued

SURFACE
❦ 10" × 12" (25.4cm × 30.5cm) piece of Winsor & Newton 140-lb. (300gsm) cold-press watercolor paper for each design

BRUSHES
❦ Loew-Cornell La Corneille series 7550, 1½-inch (38mm) wash brush
❦ Loew-Cornell Art Tec no. 4 sable
❦ Loew-Cornell Jackie Shaw no. 2 liner

ADDITIONAL SUPPLIES
❦ Masterson Sta-Wet Palette
❦ transferring supplies
❦ Krylon Workable Fixative, no. 1306
❦ two 11" × 14" (27.9cm × 35.6cm) mats with 7½" × 9½" (19.1cm × 22.9cm) openings
❦ two 11" × 14" (27.9cm × 35.6cm) frames
❦ Therm O Web Keep A Memory Acid Free Mounting Adhesive

HERB GARDEN SAMPLER

1 | *Lavender*
Basecoat the leaves and stems with Hauser Green Light, then outline and shade them with Thicket. Basecoat the upper lavender petals with Lavender and the lower petals with Purple Lilac.

2 | Shade the Lavender petals with Purple Passion and the Purple Lilac petals with Lavender.

3 | Highlight the tips of all of the petals with Lavender Sachet. Highlight the leaves and stems with Lime Yellow.

4 | *Sage*
Basecoat the leaves and stems with Hauser Green Light and shade with Thicket. Basecoat the flowers with Sterling Blue.

5 | Highlight the leaves with Lime Yellow. Shade the flowers with Heartland Blue.

6 | Add accents of Apple Spice in the darkest areas of the leaves. Highlight the tips of each flower with Baby Blue, then a dot of Wicker White.

7 | *Rosemary*
Basecoat the leaves and stems with Hauser Green Light and shade with Thicket. Basecoat the flowers with Baby Blue.

8 | Highlight the leaves and stems with Lime Yellow. Shade the flowers with Sterling Blue.

9 | Intensify the shading on the flowers with Heartland Blue. Highlight the tips of the flowers with Wicker White.

10 | Add accents of Apple Spice in the darkest areas of the leaves.

11 | *Nasturtium*
Basecoat the leaves and stems with Hauser Green Light. Shade with Thicket. Basecoat the flower centers with Turner's Yellow and the flower petals with Mix 2.

12 | Highlight the leaves and stems with Lime Yellow. Shade the flowers with Apple Spice.

13 | Highlight the flowers with Turner's Yellow. Add accents of Apple Spice in the darkest areas of the leaves.

14 | *Chives*
Basecoat the leaves and stems with Hauser Green Light and shade with Thicket. Basecoat the lower petals of the chives with Lavender and the upper petals with Lavender Sachet.

15 | Highlight the leaves and stems with Lime Yellow and shade the lower petals with Purple Passion.

16 | Highlight the lower petals with Lavender Sachet and the upper petals with Wicker White. Add accents of Apple Spice in the darkest areas of the leaves.

17 | *Marsh Mallow*
Basecoat the leaves and stems with Hauser Green Light. Shade with Thicket. Basecoat the flower centers with Turner's Yellow. Basecoat the flowers with Rose Pink.

18 | Highlight the leaves and stems with Lime Yellow. Shade the flowers with Apple Spice.

19 | Highlight the flowers with Cotton Candy. Add accents of Apple Spice in the darkest areas of the leaves.

20 | *Borage*
Basecoat the leaves and stems with Hauser Green Light. Shade with Thicket. Base the flower centers with Turner's Yellow. Base the petals with Sterling Blue and shade with Purple Passion.

21 | Highlight the leaves and stems with Lime Yellow. Highlight the tips of the petals with Baby Blue.

22 | *Chamomile*
Basecoat the leaves and stems with Hauser Green Light. Shade with Thicket and highlight with Lime Yellow. Basecoat the petals and flower centers with Turner's Yellow. Shade the centers with Turner's Yellow mixed with a touch of Purple Passion.

23 | Shade the petals with Mix 1.

24 | Highlight the petals with Wicker White. Outline the petals with Mix 1.

Mix 1 · Thicket · Heartland Blue · Purple Passion

Sage · Chamomile · Borage

Chives · Nasturtium · Rosemary · Lavender · Marsh Mallow

Purple Passion · Mix 1 · Purple Passion · Heartland Blue · Mix 1

25 | Using the no. 2 liner brush, paint the lettering with the colors indicated above. When dry, spray lightly with Krylon Workable Fixative to protect against soil and water damage.

PAINTING THE WILDFLOWER GARDEN SAMPLER

1 **Daisy**
Basecoat the leaves and stems with Hauser Green Light. Shade with Thicket. Basecoat the flower petals and centers with Turner's Yellow.

2 Highlight the leaves and stems with Lime Yellow. Shade the petals and inner flower centers with Mix 1.

3 Highlight the tips of the petals with Wicker White.

5 Highlight the leaves and stems with Lime Yellow. Highlight the flower petals with Baby Blue.

4 **Bluebell**
Basecoat the leaves and stems with Hauser Green Light. Shade with Thicket. Basecoat the flower centers with Turner's Yellow. Basecoat the inside of the flowers with Baby Blue, the main part of the flowers with Sterling Blue and the back flower petals with Purple Passion.

6 Highlight the inside sections of the flowers with Wicker White. Add accents of Apple Spice in the darkest areas of the leaves.

7 | *Lupine*
Basecoat the leaves and stems with Hauser Green Light. Shade with Thicket. Basecoat the flower centers with Turner's Yellow and the flowers with Baby Blue.

8 | Highlight the leaves and stems with Lime Yellow. Shade the flowers with Sterling Blue.

9 | Intensify the shading on the flowers with Heartland Blue.

10 | Tip the ends of the flower petals with Wicker White to highlight.

11 | *Forget-Me-Not*
Basecoat the leaves and stems with Hauser Green Light. Shade with Thicket. Basecoat the flower centers with Turner's Yellow and the flowers with Baby Blue.

12 | Highlight the leaves and stems with Lime Yellow. Shade the flowers with Sterling Blue.

13 | Intensify the shading on the flowers with Heartland Blue. Add touches of Lavender to random petals.

14 | Highlight the tips of the flower petals with Wicker White.

15 | *Viola*
Basecoat the leaves and stems with Hauser Green Light. Shade with Thicket. Basecoat the left flower with Lavender, the middle flower with Turner's Yellow and the right flower with Rose Pink.

16 | Highlight the leaves and stems with Lime Yellow. Shade the left flower with Heartland Blue and base the center with Turner's Yellow. Shade the middle flower with Mix 2 and base the center with Heartland Blue. Shade the right flower with Apple Spice and base the center with Turner's Yellow.

17 | Highlight the left flower with Lavender Sachet, the middle flower with Wicker White, and the right flower with Cotton Candy.

19 | Highlight the leaves and stems with Lime Yellow. Shade the left and right flowers with Apple Spice and the middle flower with Purple Passion.

18 | *Wild Geranium*
Basecoat the leaves and stems with Hauser Green Light. Shade with Thicket. Basecoat the left and right flowers with Rose Pink. Basecoat the middle flower with Lavender, except the turned portion of the petal, which is base-coated with Lavender Sachet.

20 | Highlight the flowers with Wicker White.

21 | *Cosmos*
Basecoat the leaves and stems with Hauser Green Light. Shade with Thicket. Basecoat the flower centers with Turner's Yellow. Basecoat the bottom flowers with Rose Pink and the top flower with Turner's Yellow.

22 | Shade the flowers with Apple Spice.

23 | Highlight the leaves and stems with Lime Yellow. Highlight the flowers with Wicker White.

24 | Add accents of Apple Spice in the darkest areas of the leaves.

Mix 1 — Purple Passion — Mix 1 — Heartland Blue

Wild Geranium

Daisy

Wild Lupine

Wildflower Garden

Bluebell

Viola

Forget Me Not

Cosmos

Michelle Temous

Purple Passion — Heartland Blue — Thicket — Mix 1

25 | Using the no. 2 liner brush, paint the lettering with the colors indicated above. When dry, spray lightly with Krylon Workable Fixative to protect against soil and water damage.

Feverfew & Chicory

I painted these two designs on Barb Watson's wonderful, preprimed metal plates. No prep work is required and the smooth surface of the plates is luxurious to paint on.

These designs feature a color scheme loosely based on the

Provence region of France. The climate there is hot and sunny, and brightly colored cotton print dresses in blue, yellow and red are part of the traditional costume.

If you sneak a peek at an artist's color wheel, you will see that this color scheme works so beautifully because it is based on a classic color triad.

Plaid FolkArt Acrylic Paints

Black Cherry	Apple Spice	Glazed Carrots	Turner's Yellow (Artists' Pigment)	Lemonade
Hauser Green Dark (Artists' Pigment)	Hauser Green Medium (Artists' Pigment)	Hauser Green Light (Artists' Pigment)	Lime Yellow	
Blue Ink	Heartland Blue	Sterling Blue	Light Periwinkle	Baby Blue
Dioxazine Purple (Artists' Pigment)	Lavender	Orchid		
Aqua (Artists' Pigment)	Wicker White			

Materials continued on page 98.

Feverfew

© 2000 Michelle Temares

This pattern may be hand-traced or photocopied for personal
use only. Enlarge at 167% to return to full size.

Chicory

© 2000 Michelle Temares

This pattern may be hand-traced or photocopied for personal
use only. Shown at full size. Use the border pattern from page
96 for the rim of this plate.

PREPARING THE PLATE BACKGROUNDS

Use the no. 4 sable for all steps except for the lettering, which is painted with a no. 2 liner.

Materials, continued

SURFACE

❧ These 12-inch (30.5cm) diameter wooden plates are available from:
Barb Watson's Brushworks
P.O. Box 1467
Moreno, CA 92556
Phone: (909) 653-3780
Web site: www.barbwatson.com

BRUSHES

❧ Loew-Cornell Art Tec no. 4 sable
❧ Loew-Cornell Jackie Shaw no. 2 liner

ADDITIONAL SUPPLIES

❧ Masterson Sta-Wet Palette
❧ transferring supplies
❧ two 8" × 10" (20.3cm × 25.4cm) pieces of cheesecloth
❧ FolkArt Blending Gel
❧ FolkArt Artists' Varnish, matte

1 Basecoat the rim of both plates with two coats of Heartland Blue and the centers with two coats of Turner's Yellow.

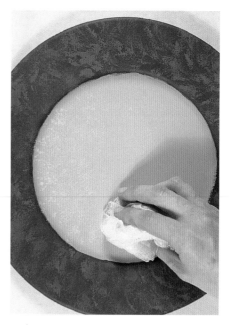

2 On your palette, prepare a mix of 1 part Sterling Blue and 1 part Blending Gel.

3 Loosely scrunch up an 8" × 10" (20.3cm × 25.4cm) piece of cheesecloth, and dip it lightly into the blending gel mix. Lightly touch the paint-dipped cheesecloth to the plate rim, working your way around the entire rim. Lift the cloth and turn your wrist repeatedly so that the texture pattern is varied.

4 On your palette, prepare a mix of 1 part Lemonade and 1 part Blending Gel. Touch this mixture into the center of both plates using the same technique as in step 3.

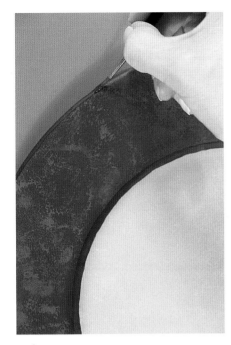

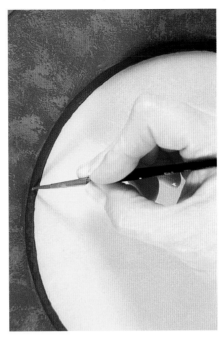

5 | Paint a border along the inner rim and along the outer edge with Black Cherry.

6 | Make a mix of 1 part Apple Spice and 1 part Blending Gel. Since these areas are too narrow for the cheesecloth technique, use your brush to randomly dab this color over the Black Cherry rim and border.

PAINTING THE BORDERS FOR BOTH PLATES

1 | Basecoat all of the leaves with Hauser Green Medium.

2 | *Nasturtium*
Basecoat the centers with Lemonade. Basecoat the flowers with Glazed Carrots. Shade the flowers with Apple Spice. Shade the leaves with Hauser Green Dark.

3 | Highlight the flowers with Lemon-ade and the leaves with Hauser Green Light.

4 | Intensify the highlights on the leaves with Lime Yellow. Add accents of Apple Spice in the darkest areas of the leaves.

5 | *Sage*
Basecoat the flowers with Light Periwinkle. Shade with Blue Ink. Shade the leaves with Hauser Green Dark.

6 | Highlight the flowers with Baby Blue and the leaves with Hauser Green Light.

7 | Intensify the leaf highlights with Lime Yellow and the flower petal highlights with small dots of Wicker White. Add accents of Apple Spice in the darkest areas of the leaves.

8 | *Chamomile*
Basecoat the flowers with Aqua plus a touch of Glazed Carrots. Shade the leaves with Hauser Green Dark and the flowers with Blue Ink. Base the centers with Lemonade.

9 | Highlight the leaves with Hauser Green Light and the flowers with Baby Blue. Shade the centers with Turner's Yellow.

10 | Intensify the highlights on the leaves with Lime Yellow. Add accents of Apple Spice in the darkest areas of the leaves.

11 | *Lavender*
Basecoat the flowers with Lavender. Shade with Dioxazine Purple. Shade the leaves with Hauser Green Dark.

12 | Highlight the leaves with Hauser Green Light. Highlight the flower petals with a small dot of Orchid.

13 | Intensify the highlights on the leaves with Lime Yellow. Add a dot of Wicker White to the center of the Lavender petals to highlight.

14 | Add accents of Apple Spice in the darkest areas of the leaves.

PAINTING THE FEVERFEW

1 | Basecoat the flower centers with Lemonade. Basecoat the leaves with Hauser Green Medium. With Hauser Green Dark, shade from the outside edges of the leaves in and along the center veins.

2 | Highlight the leaves with Hauser Green Light. Basecoat the ladybug's body with Apple Spice and its head with Dioxazine Purple.

3 | Intensify the highlights on the leaves with Lime Yellow. Add the ladybug's legs and spots with Dioxazine Purple. Accent the leaves with Apple Spice.

4 | Basecoat the flowers with Wicker White. Draw a very thin line of Hauser Green Light between the petals to separate.

5 | At the ends of each petal, paint a small dash of Turner's Yellow.

6 | Using the liner brush, paint in the lettering with thinned Hauser Green Dark.

7 | Wash all of the flowers with a watery wash of Lemonade.

M. Yeadon Feverfew

8 | Protect with three coats of matte varnish.

Painting the Chicory

1 | Basecoat the leaves with Hauser Green Medium and shade with Hauser Green Dark.

2 | Highlight the leaves with Hauser Green Light.

3 | Add accents of Apple Spice in the darkest areas of the leaves.

4 | Basecoat the flowers with Baby Blue and shade with Light Periwinkle. Basecoat the butterfly's body with Blue Ink.

5 | Shade the flowers with Blue Ink.

6 | Highlight the tips of the flower petals with Wicker White. Base the flower centers with Lemonade and shade with Turner's Yellow.

7 | Basecoat the top of the butterfly with Lime Yellow and shade with Light Periwinkle. Basecoat the bottom of the butterfly with Orchid and shade with Lavender.

8 | Shade the top of the butterfly again with Blue Ink and the bottom with Dioxazine Purple.

9 | Finish the butterfly with Wicker White highlights.

10 | Using the liner brush, paint in the lettering with thinned Hauser Green Dark. Protect with three coats of matte varnish.

Chicory

Peony

Every year I eagerly look forward to May, when the peonies will bloom in my garden. Peonies seem to be a perfect flower: Their showy beauty is difficult to surpass, they smell heavenly, they make long-lasting cut flowers, and they are easy to grow.

In its native land of China, the peony is a symbol of luck and prosperity. If you do not have the opportunity to grow peonies in a garden, paint this lovely tray, and may they forever bring luck and prosperity into your home.

Plaid FolkArt Acrylic Paints

Mix 1 Fuchsia + a touch of Hauser Green Dark	Mix 2 1 part Light Fuchsia + 1 part Fuchsia	Mix 3 1 part Bright Baby Pink + 1 part Fuchsia	Mix 4 1 part Bright Baby Pink + 1 part Icy White
Lavender	Violet Pansy	Mix 5 4 parts Icy White + 1 part Red Violet	
Hauser Green Dark (Artists' Pigment)	Hauser Green Light (Artists' Pigment)	Lime Yellow	
Aspen Green	Mystic Green	Mix 6 3 parts Icy White + 1 part Mystic Green	
Antique Gold (Metallics)	Icy White		

Materials continued on page 109.

© 2000 Michelle Temares

This pattern may be hand-traced or photocopied for personal use only. Enlarge at 153% to bring it up to full size.

Paint all of the following steps with the no. 4 round.

1 Spread an even layer of Blending Gel over the sealed and sanded surface of the tray. Drop alternating, random blobs of Lime Yellow and Hauser Green Light paint onto the tray surface. Gather a handful of plastic wrap into a loose ball. Twist the plastic wrap down into the paint and lift repeatedly until the surface is blended. Allow to dry thoroughly.

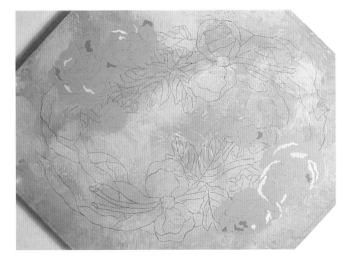

2 When basecoating the peonies, keep the paint transparent enough that the transfer lines show through; this will eliminate the need to retransfer the lines after you basecoat. The lines will be covered by the subsequent shading and highlighting. Basecoat the main petals of the peonies with Mix 3, the turned petals with Mix 4 and the inside petals with Mix 2.

3 Shade the main peony petals with Mix 2 and the light petals with Mix 3.

4 | Deepen the shading with Mix 1.

5 | Highlight the petals with Mix 4.

6 | Block in the stems and the center of the left side of the leaves with Lime Yellow. Surround the Lime Yellow with Mix 6 and place Mystic Green toward the edges.

7 Block in the right side of the leaves with Mix 6 in the center, surrounded by Mystic Green, then Aspen Green toward the edges.

8 Paint in vein lines with Mystic Green on the left side of the leaves and Aspen Green on the right side of the leaves.

9 Drybrush highlights in the leaf centers. Use Mix 6 on the left side of the leaves and Mystic Green on the right side of the leaves. Reinforce the dark areas with small accents of Hauser Green Dark.

10 | Block in the ribbon with Lavender. Shade the underneath portions of the ribbon with Violet Pansy and highlight the overlapping sections with Mix 5.

11 | Drybrush highlights in the center of the ribbon with Mix 5 and then Mix 4. Accent the very lightest portions with small amounts of Icy White.

12 | Drybrush accents of Lavender on random petals.

13 | Paint the bow handles with three coats of Metallic Antique Gold. Finish the tray with matte varnish.

Iris & Columbine

Among the earliest botanical florals are those found in the margins of Europe's illuminated manuscripts from the Middle Ages. The term "illuminated" referred to the gold or silver metals used in the painting to catch the light—or illuminate—the page.

Illuminated manuscripts were frequently religious texts. Earthly motifs, such as flowers and insects, were popular subjects.

The original illuminated manuscripts were written on papyrus. Later, more sturdy parchment was the surface of choice. Although we will be painting on watercolor paper, this project has the look and feel of aged parchment due to the techniques used to paint the background.

Plaid FolkArt Acrylic Paints

Apple Spice	Glazed Carrots	Pure Gold (Metallic)	
English Mustard	Yellow Ochre (Artists' Pigment)	Buttercup	
Thicket	Hauser Green Medium (Artists' Pigment)	Hauser Green Light (Artists' Pigment)	Lime Yellow
Periwinkle	Light Periwinkle	Baby Blue	
Red Violet	Heather	Violet Pansy	Mix 1 5 parts Wicker White + 1 part Heather

Materials continued on page 118.

© 2000 Michelle Temares

This pattern may be hand-traced or photocopied for personal use only. Enlarge at 155% on a photocopier to return to full size.

Columbine

This pattern may be hand-traced or photocopied for personal
use only. Shown at full size. Use the border pattern from page
117 for this design.

In the following demonstration, I will be painting both the iris and columbine designs simultaneously. The steps are the same for both designs unless otherwise indicated. You can paint these designs one at a time if you prefer. Paint all of the following steps with the no. 4 sable, except where indicated in the instructions.

Materials, continued

SURFACE

❦ 13" × 16" (33cm × 40.6cm) piece of Winsor & Newton 140-lb. (300gsm) cold-press watercolor paper for each design

BRUSHES

❦ Loew-Cornell Art Tec no. 4 sable
❦ Loew-Cornell series 7520, ¼-inch (6mm) rake brush

ADDITIONAL SUPPLIES

❦ Masterson Sta-Wet Palette
❦ transferring supplies
❦ Krylon Workable Fixative, no. 1306
❦ scissors and scrap paper
❦ old toothbrush
❦ two 14" × 18" (35.6cm × 46cm) mats with 9¾" × 12¾" (25cm × 32.4cm) openings
❦ two 14" × 18" (35.6cm × 46cm) frames
❦ Therm O Web Keep a Memory Acid Free Mounting Adhesive

1 │ Basecoat the center rectangle with Buttercup and the widest border background with Yellow Ochre.

2 │ Cut pieces of scrap paper to fit over the center and the decorative initial square to protect them. Dip an old toothbrush into thinned English Mustard. Spatter the outer border by running your thumb against the toothbrush.

3 │ Mask out everything but the center rectangle with scrap paper. Spatter with thinned Yellow Ochre.

4 | Load the ¼-inch (6mm) rake brush with thinned Yellow Ochre. Spread the bristles apart by pressing down on the palette. Draw the brush randomly across the background of the center rectangle. Repeat with thinned English Mustard on the background of the widest border.

5 | Paint the border closest to the center rectangle and the decorative initial with Pure Gold. Paint the outermost border and the border next to the gold border with Periwinkle.

6 | Using the point of your no. 4 sable brush, dot in Pure Gold between the larger dots on the inner Periwinkle border.

7 | Alternate with dots of Apple Spice and Hauser Green Light to fill in the larger dots.

8 | Basecoat the background of the border next to the outer Periwinkle border with Baby Blue.

9 | Paint in the stems on the Baby Blue border with Hauser Green Light. Paint push-pull leaves alternating between Hauser Green Light and Hauser Green Medium. Indicate vein lines with Hauser Green Light on the medium leaves and Hauser Green Medium on the light leaves.

10 Basecoat the circle motifs with Buttercup. Paint in the lines on the circles with Apple Spice and the leaves with Periwinkle. Add Apple Spice and Baby Blue push-pull flowers to the border.

11 With thinned Periwinkle, paint a thin line between the Baby Blue and Pure Gold borders.

12 Basecoat the stem around the decorative intial with Hauser Green Medium, the flowers with Light Periwinkle and the background with Apple Spice.

13 Highlight the flowers with Baby Blue and the stem with Hauser Green Light and Lime Yellow. Shade the stem with Thicket.

14 Basecoat all the leaves and stems on the wide Pure Gold border with Lime Yellow. Working wet-in-wet, shade the leaves and stems with Hauser Green Light and then Hauser Green Medium.

15 Basecoat the backgrounds of the medallions on the gold border with Buttercup. Basecoat the medallion borders with Baby Blue. Working wet-in-wet, shade the borders with Light Periwinkle, then Periwinkle.

16 | Basecoat the lily petals with Buttercup. While this color is still wet, blend in Glazed Carrots.

17 | Continuing to work wet-in-wet on the lilies, blend in Apple Spice.

18 | Basecoat the border irises with Heather, shade with Violet Pansy, then deepen the shade with Red Violet. Basecoat the beards on the irises with Buttercup and shade with Yellow Ochre.

20 | Basecoat the upper ruffled edges of the wings of the butterfly on the left side of the border with Baby Blue. Shade with Light Periwinkle. Basecoat the lower ruffled edges of the wings with Heather and shade with Red Violet. Basecoat the body and lower wings with Baby Blue and shade with Light Periwinkle. Basecoat the upper wings with Buttercup and shade with Hauser Green Medium. Outline the body and paint in the antenne with Red Violet. Paint the dots on the wings with Periwinkle, then add Red Violet dots in the centers.

19 | Drybrush Baby Blue highlights on the centers of the iris petals.

21 | Basecoat the tips of the upper wings on the butterfly on the right side of the border with Light Periwinkle. Shade with Periwinkle. Basecoat the tips of the lower wings with Heather and shade with Red Violet. Basecoat the upper wings with Buttercup and shade with Heather. Basecoat the lower wings with Buttercup and shade with Hauser Green Medium. Paint in the antennae with Red Violet. Basecoat the body with Periwinkle and shade with Red Violet.

22 | Basecoat the body and inner section of the wings of the butterfly in the medallion with Heather, then shade with Red Violet. Paint in Red Violet dots with Periwinkle centers. Basecoat the back wings with Baby Blue and shade with Light Periwinkle, then Periwinkle. Basecoat the front wings with Baby Blue. Shade with Light Periwinkle, then Periwinkle. Basecoat the ruffles with Heather and shade with Red Violet.

23 | Basecoat the outer petals of the columbines in the border with Baby Blue. Shade with Light Periwinkle, then Periwinkle. Outline the outer petals with Periwinkle. Basecoat the inner petals with Heather. Shade with Violet Pansy, then Red Violet, and outline these petals with Red Violet.

24 | Work in sections to paint the birds, allowing each area to dry before moving on to the next. Basecoat the birds with Baby Blue. Shade with Light Periwinkle, then Periwinkle. Add small accents of Red Violet. Paint the beaks and legs with Buttercup, then shade with Red Violet. Paint the branch with English Mustard and shade with Apple Spice.

25 | Basecoat the round daisy on the left side of the decorative initial with Buttercup. Shade with Glazed Carrots and Apple Spice, allowing the brush marks to show. Basecoat the round daisy at the top of the border (shown on page 125) with Heather, shade with Violet Pansy and drybrush Baby Blue in the center of each petal.

26 | Basecoat the tulip at the upper left-hand corner of the decorative initial (shown in previous step) with Baby Blue, shade with Light Periwinkle, then Periwinkle. Basecoat the tulip at the bottom left of the border with Buttercup, then shade with Glazed Carrots and Apple Spice. Basecoat the tulip on the right side of the border (shown on page 125) with Buttercup and shade with Light Periwinkle, then Violet Pansy.

27 | Basecoat the front leaves on the center irises with Lime Yellow. Shade with Hauser Green Light, then Hauser Green Medium, and accent with Buttercup. Basecoat the back leaves with Hauser Green Light. Shade with Hauser Green Medium, then Thicket.

28 | Basecoat the center irises with Heather and shade with Violet Pansy, then Red Violet. Accent the edges of the petals with Baby Blue. Basecoat the beards with Buttercup, shade with Yellow Ochre and add small accents of Apple Spice. Paint in the lettering with thinned Red Violet.

29 | Basecoat the leaves and stems on the center columbine with Hauser Green Light. Shade with Hauser Green Medium, then Thicket.

30 | Highlight the center of the leaves and stems with Hauser Green Light, then Lime Yellow. Add veins to the leaves with Hauser Green Medium.

31 | Basecoat the purple columbines with Heather and shade with Violet Pansy, then Red Violet. Highlight with Mix 1. Paint the lettering with thinned Red Violet.

32 | Highlight the purple columbines with Baby Blue and tip the edges with Mix 1.

33 | Basecoat the blue columbine with Baby Blue and shade with Light Periwinkle.

34 | Add a deeper shade with Periwinkle.

35 | Reinforce the dark areas of the blue columbine with Red Violet and the dark areas of the purple columbines with Periwinkle.

36 When the paintings are thoroughly dry, spray each lightly with Krylon Workable Fixative to protect against water damage and dirt.

Resources

ALTO'S EZ MAT, INC.

607 W. Third Ave.
Ellensburg, WA 98926
Phone: (800) 225-2497
Web site: www.altosezmat.com
(Alto's 4501 Mat Cutting System and
Alto's 4505 Deluxe Mat Cutting
System)

BARB WATSON'S BRUSHWORKS

P.O. Box 1467
Moreno Valley, CA 92556
Phone: (909) 653-3780
Fax: (909) 653-5573
Web site: www.barbwatson.com
(project 3 metal bowl and project 6
metal plates)

**CRESCENT CARDBOARD
COMPANY, L.L.C.**

100 W. Willow Rd.
Wheeling, IL 60090
Phone: (800) 323-1055
Fax: (847) 537-7153
Web site:
www.crescent-cardboard.com
(mat board)

HY-JO PICTURE FRAMES

P.O. Box 646
Lawrenceville, GA 30246
Phone: (770) 963-5256
(picture frames used in finished
project shots)

KRYLON

Phone: (800) 4 KRYLON
Web site: www.krylon.com
(Krylon Workable Fixative,
no. 1306)

LOEW-CORNELL

563 Chestnut Ave.
Teaneck, NJ 07666-2490
Phone: (201) 836-7070
Fax: (201) 836-8110
Web site: www.loew-cornell.com
E-mail:
loew-cornell@loew-cornell.com
(Loew-Cornell Art Tec and La
Corneille brushes)

**MASTERSON ART
PRODUCTS, INC.**

P.O. Box 10775
Glendale, AZ 85318
Phone: (800) 965-2675
Web site: www.mastersonart.com
E-mail: info@mastersonart.com
(Masterson Sta-Wet Palette)

PLAID ENTERPRISES, INC.

Attn: Customer Service
P.O. Box 2835
Norcross, GA 30091-2835
Phone: (800) 842-4197
Web site: www.plaidonline.com
E-mail: talk@plaidonline.com
(FolkArt acrylic paints, Blending Gel
and Artists' Varnish)

THERM O WEB, INC.

770 Glenn Ave.
Wheeling, IL 60090
Phone: (847) 520-5200
Fax: (847) 520-0025
Web site: www.thermoweb.com
(Keep A Memory Acid Free
Mounting Adhesive)

VIKING WOODCRAFTS

1317 Eighth St. SE
Waseca, MN 56093
Phone: (507) 835-8043
Web site: www.vikingwoodcrafts.com
(project 7 wooden tray)

WALNUT HOLLOW FARM, INC.

1409 State Rd. 23
Dodgeville, WI 53533
Phone: (800) 950-5101
Web site: www.walnuthollow.com
(hobby wood embellishments
for frames)

WINSOR & NEWTON

U.S. and Canadian residents:
P.O. Box 1396
Piscataway, NJ 08855
For contacts in all other parts of
the globe:
Whitefriars Ave.
Harrow, Middlesex HA3 5RH
England
Web site: www.winsornewton.com
(140-lb. [300gsm] cold-press water-
color paper)

The following Canadian retailers may also carry the supplies used in this book:

CRAFTS CANADA

2745 Twenty-ninth St. NE
Calgary, Ontario T1Y 7B5

FOLK ART ENTERPRISES

P.O. Box 1088
Ridgetown, Ontario N0P 2C0
Phone: (888) 214-0062

MACPHERSON CRAFT WHOLESALE

83 Queen St. E.
P.O. Box 1870
St. Mary's, Ontario N4X 1C2
Phone: (519) 284-1741

MAUREEN MCNAUGHTON ENTERPRISES

RR #2
Belwood, Ontario N0B 1J0
Phone: (519) 843-5648

MERCURY ART & CRAFT SUPERSHOP

332 Wellington St.
London, Ontario N6C 4P7
Phone: (519) 434-1636

TOWN & COUNTRY FOLK ART SUPPLIES

93 Green Lane
Thornhill, Ontario L3T 6K6
Phone: (905) 882-0199

Metric Conversion Chart

to convert	to	multiply by
Inches	Centimeters	2.54
Centimeters	Inches	0.4
Feet	Centimeters	30.5
Centimeters	Feet	0.03
Yards	Meters	0.9
Meters	Yards	1.1
Sq. Inches	Sq. Centimeters	6.45
Sq. Centimeters	Sq. Inches	0.16
Sq. Feet	Sq. Meters	0.09
Sq. Meters	Sq. Feet	10.8
Sq. Yards	Sq. Meters	0.8
Sq. Meters	Sq. Yards	1.2
Pounds	Kilograms	0.45
Kilograms	Pounds	2.2
Ounces	Grams	28.4
Grams	Ounces	0.04

INDEX